JOURNEY NOTES

*Writing for Recovery
and Spiritual Growth*

About the Authors: Richard Solly of St. Paul, Minnesota, received the 1988-89 Pearl Hogrefe Fellowship in creative writing from Iowa State University and has won the Minneapolis-based Loft Mentor Series, as well as grants from the Minnesota State Arts Board. His own journal, *Days and Nights,* was serialized in *The Phoenix,* a literary publication in Massachusetts. He has taught creative writing in Minnesota Writers-in-the-Schools, Artists-in-Education, and led numerous writing workshops for older adults and disabled people. He has written a number of pamphlets for Hazelden and currently teaches at the Loft.

Roseann Lloyd is one of the authors of the book, *Today's Gift: Daily Meditations for Families,* published by Hazelden Educational Materials. Her first book of poetry is *Tap Dancing for Big Mom.* Her poems are included in the new anthology *Minnesota Writes: Poetry,* published by Milkweed Editions, and in many literary journals. She is the co-translator of *The House with the Blind Glass Windows,* the story of a girl coming of age in an alcoholic family, which was published by Seal Press in 1987. She completed an M.A. at the University of Minnesota and has studied poetry at the University of Montana with Tess Gallagher and Richard Hugo. Lloyd lives in Minneapolis and teaches writing. She also does work as a writing consultant for groups and individuals.

JOURNEY NOTES

Writing for Recovery and Spiritual Growth

RICHARD SOLLY
ROSEANN LLOYD

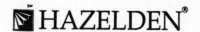

HAZELDEN®

First published August 1989

ISBN: 0-89486-606-0
Library of Congress Catalog Card Number: 89-83557

Printed in the United States of America.

This book is dedicated to
Rose Ellen Solly
and
Anna Rachel Genich
for being who they are

Contents

Preface

We have both been writing off and on most of our lives, sometimes publicly, always privately. Notes from our journeys are scattered all over: in journals and notebooks, in boxes of scraps stored in attics, in file folders stacked on shelves, in old briefcases. Many of our notes didn't survive and filled up wastebaskets.

For the last ten years, we have also been teaching creative writing to adults and children. As writing teachers, we've seen the healing power of writing in some of our students' lives. We decided to write this book as a way to talk about writing as a process for getting clarity, balance, and honesty, for dealing with difficult issues.

"Writing isn't the same thing as therapy, but it is healing in and of itself. It is a process where you begin to take your feelings and arrange them, as if you were making a quilt," wrote Minneapolis writer Nora Reza recently. We agree with the important distinction this quote makes between writing and therapy. Writing can never take the place of therapy or other important activities, such as group meetings, intimate human relationships, conscious spiritual practices, and a healthy lifestyle.

We hope this book will be useful for people in recovery programs, as well as for those who simply enjoy writing. We are using the word *recovery* in the broad sense, believing that all of us have recovery work to do. Divorce, deaths in families, illnesses, separations, unemployment, as well as alcoholism, other drug addiction, and codependency, call forth the desire for clarity and serenity. We have included in the book writing exercises that we believe best deal with these concerns. The exercises designed for working the Twelve Steps may also be adapted and used by people who are not in a Twelve Step program.

We've written this book so anyone can use it. Some people write for themselves, privately, and have no desire to go on to become writers. Others want to go on, take writing classes, and develop into poets and fiction writers. Because this book is for everyone, we have included writing from beginning level students and renowned prize-winning poets and writers. Some of the writers are in a Twelve Step program and some are not. The anonymity of the Twelve Step program writers is protected, for the most part, by the use of their first names only. In some cases, a person requested that no name be used. Some writers have already chosen to break their anonymity and have spoken publicly about their recovery; these people are identified by their full names at their request.

Sometimes counselors and therapists have asked us how they can encourage clients to explore personal issues through writing. We suggest they can learn about this process by starting a journal themselves and working through some of the exercises in this book to see which ones are applicable to their clients. It is easier to encourage others to write when you know yourself the thrills and difficulties of writing.

Our hope for the book is simple: that we might all live happier lives.

We want to thank all of the contributors to the book for sharing their most intimate writings with the world.

We especially want to send our thanks to Gary Kern and Karen Shaud, to our friends and families who have been with us as the book unfolded, to our students, to our original editor at Hazelden, Terry Spohn, and current editor, Rebecca Post. Finally, we want to thank the anonymous people in the Twelve Step programs for their courage and generosity.

Acknowledgments

We thank the writers, editors and publishers who granted us permission to reprint the following materials:

Breckenridge, Jill, "My Mother's Hands," and "Poetry as Connection," from *The Great River Review*, Volume 6, Number 2, 1985. Copyright © 1985 by Jill Breckenridge. Reprinted by permission of the author. "Prayer Asking for Blessing on Creative Work," from *The Phoenix*, June, 1988. Copyright © 1988 by Jill Breckenridge. Reprinted by permission of the author.

Bridges, Grace Caroline, "straight/not straight," from *Evergreen Chronicles*, Volume 3, Number 4, Summer, 1988. Copyright © 1988 by Grace Caroline Bridges. Reprinted by permission of the author.

Carver, Raymond, "Fear," from *Where Water Comes Together With Other Water* by Raymond Carver. Published by Random House in 1984. Copyright © 1984 by Raymond Carver.

Day, Sharon, "The Chartings," appeared in *Drink the winds, Let the waters flow free*, The Johnson Institute, 1983. Copyright © 1983 by Sharon Day. Reprinted by permission of the author.

Green, Kate, "Don't Make Your Life Too Beautiful," from *If the World Is Running Out*, Holy Cow! Press, 1983. Copyright © 1983 by Kate Green. Reprinted by permission of Holy Cow! Press.

CHAPTER 1

The Lock and the Key: Journal Writing

All of writing is a huge lake...all that matters is feeding the lake.

— Jean Rhys

Some record only what has happened to them; but others how they have happened to the universe.

— Henry David Thoreau

The psychoanalyst, Carl Jung, once described an ancient ritual where a spellbinding circle was drawn for protection. Drawing a circle has been used "since olden times to set a place apart as holy and inviolable..." This circle was called a sacred *tenemous*. Everyone inside it was temporarily suspended from all responsibilities. They were left there to dream, to idle, to meditate, to do whatever they pleased. Once outside the circle, their daily lives and burdens were resumed, but inside the *tenemous* they were free from the ordinary duties of life. Another ritual can be found among some Native American people who use a sacred sweat lodge in a similar way. Inside the shelter, they meditated, dreamed, and had visions. In a similar way, the journal can be a *tenemous*.

A journal is a safe and private place. It's an *inviolate* place that lets us observe life, reflect, dream, and express our feelings and thoughts. While we are writing, the journal lets us escape the world's tedium.

In the hustle and bustle of our daily lives, we don't often have time to reflect on what we are doing or why we are doing it. Introspection isn't encouraged in our society, which seems to value activities that are more functional. Writing helps us keep in touch with ourselves in a technological era that shows far more interest in outer space than the inner space of a notebook. Journals and diaries let us take a deep breath of air and meditate, reflect, or simply muse.

Best Friends

Journals and diaries can be workshops for the soul, laboratories where we can investigate and examine our lives, our secrets, hurts, resentments, memories, and joys. Journals are records for the heart and mind. They chart the joys and sorrows of our daily lives, and, like road maps, they can direct us back to our hearts after confusing experiences. Journals are testaments of our lives, that we live as fully and consciously as we can. Without journals, certain experiences and episodes discovered through writing and communicating with our deeper selves would be lost. These experiences that lay deep in our souls are too important to be forgotten. We owe it to ourselves to remember them, to write them down, to relish and learn from them. We are the only ones who have our particular memories and experiences. If they aren't written down, they will be forgotten and lost in an abyss.

The whole point of keeping a diary is that we might live more joyously, accepting even the pain, and in this inner laboratory of the journal, transmute our experiences into wisdom.

Diaries and journals have often been described as our best friends. Most often, we feel free to speak our minds to our friends, and when we are in trouble, they will be there to listen. Similarly, our journals are always available to us when we need them. They will not scold us for writing our deepest regrets, angers, or shames. They are there. Listening and accepting. They will not frown or turn their backs on us. We are free to say and write anything we want. What we hesitate to say to someone at work we are free to write in our journals. The anger, or even the joy, we feel at home with our spouses but never express, we are free to write about in journals. What we concealed from our parents as children, we are free to describe in our diaries. And most importantly, what we deny and hide from ourselves, we are free to explore and rediscover.

A Safe Place

Patricia Hampl, poet and author of numerous books, once wrote in an essay, *A Book with a Lock and a Key*, "Anyone can write a diary. It, even more than letters, is the least literary of forms, the most open to idiosyncrasy and innovation....I have always kept a journal myself, at least intermittently. It seemed to be instinctive."

People in all walks of life are writing in diaries and journals. In the last twenty years, an increasing interest in journals or diaries has grown. The success of Anaïs Nin's diaries, shows that journals appeal to a wide range of people. After author, therapist, and lecturer Ira Progoff, using Nin's diaries as a springboard, developed the "Intensive Journal Workshop," people who had secretly kept journals or diaries for years responded with enthusiasm. Therapists and counselors suggest that their clients keep a journal. A fourth grade teacher asks a class of students to keep a diary. Fiction writers and poets use journals as a type of workbook. A farmer religiously records the weather or the growth of his or her crops. Some nurses, doctors, mechanical engineers, blue collar workers, and students either keep a journal or know someone who does.

Diaries have become valuable tools in self-help programs. Because journals and diaries provide a safe place to explore ourselves, people in crisis, such as those in chemical dependency treatment, often turn to journals and writing in hope of mapping out their problems and finding solutions. They're used by a variety of people out of an inner desire to write. Today, writing in journals or writing creative nonfiction and memoirs has become a valid, literary genre.

Many books that we think of as finished works were originally journals, such as *Give Us Each Day: The Diary of Alice Dunbar Nelson*. Another example is *An Interrupted Life* by Ettie Hillsum. Perhaps the most famous American journal is Thoreau's *Walden Pond*. There is a strong tradition in America to write about nature and spirituality together using the less formal structure of a journal. *Pilgrim At Tinker Creek*, by Annie Dilliard, is an example. May Sarton's journals are also good examples of how journals might serve a person spiritually.

Author Patricia Hampl had this to say about journals:

> I believe there has to be a place where you can talk to yourself and know you are alone. It's beautiful...the start of the journey itself, each person's journey, each person's journal. I love that Russian custom in the old novels, where, before setting out on a long journey, the travelers sit down for a few minutes to "collect themselves." During each day there should be this "sitting," our coats buttoned against the cold we must face, the journal open on the table before us.
> — Patricia Hampl

Choosing Your Journal

Some people draw a careful distinction between diaries and journals. Journals are often identified as having greater depth of feeling and reflection. Some people think the term diaries is "school-girlish," a simple and boring record of facts.

However, many people are comfortable with either term and use them interchangeably to describe their notebooks. As authors, we don't feel a distinction needs to be drawn and we will also use the words interchangeably. *What you write* in the notebook is important, *not what you call it.*

We define journals here broadly. Journal writing involves more than the traditional diary with a lock and key. Diaries and journals can include anything written on scraps of paper, loose-leaf pages, or backs of envelopes. A journal might be typed on a computer. A diary could be a collection of eight-by-eleven-inch loose-leaf papers tossed in a single drawer week after week, or notes and reflections hastily jotted down on a small pad kept in your back pocket. Once a journal is broadly defined in this manner, many of our students proclaim, "Oh, sure, I've done that. I just never thought of that scrap paper I saved as a journal."

Some diarists draw pictures throughout their notebooks, others paste them in, and some might illustrate what they write with cartoons. The real challenge to diarists is to discover how they want to keep their own diary. For someone who prefers innovative methods, a traditional diary or a notebook with blank pages and a cloth marker might be too formal. On the other hand, for someone who prefers structure, a more traditional diary with dates and page numbers might be appealing. One writer, taking advantage of the piles of *National Geographic* his father had stored in the basement, would cut out an appealing picture, lay it over the cover of his notebook, and then cover it with clear contact paper. Looking back at past volumes, the writer can easily identify the period he wrote by the picture on the front of the book. For other writers, this process may be too complicated; they may prefer a simple spiral-bound notebook. The secret is to find your own style.

Different Ways to Use Journals

Besides the variety of ways to design your journal, there are a variety of ways to use a diary. Some professional writers use their journals to keep themselves writing daily. It disciplines them. Some fiction writers jot down ideas for future stories, as well as stories that never get written. They might take careful notes in their journals about overheard conversations to use later as dialogue. Poets might use journals to write down images that come to them spontaneously. A businessman working for a high tech industrial company might use his diary to record fantasies and feelings that he can't seem to express otherwise. Some people use journals as sounding boards, to complain, gripe, swear, and to get things off their chests. Some write for recovery and use diaries as a way to explore their lives. Therapists or counselors can use them for themselves, as well as for their clients. Some use journals to record dreams. These notebooks could be called *dream-journals*. Others use journals to explore their understanding of God. "Dear God," may begin their journal entries.

Journals or diaries can be used to monitor behavior we want to let go of. For example, we might wish to stop smoking and write in our journals when we smoke, when the urge is strongest, and how much we smoke. The journal helps us observe our behavior patterns.

We find travel diaries kept on long journeys. Letter diaries comprised of letters a person might write to a particular person, a child, a parent, friend, or even a stranger. There are cabin diaries, notebooks left in cabins or historical inns that visitors are encouraged to read and write in. There are family journals or open diaries. These are journals left in some conspicuous place like on the living room table. Each member of the family writes in the journal anytime they want. They can also read it whenever they please. Some of these open diaries can be found in halfway houses in which the residents are encouraged to write.

Some people use two journals, one to record the factual things they do in a day, and the other to record thoughts, feelings, and reflections. One student kept a "shadow diary," a second diary he kept hidden because it contained "secrets" and feelings he couldn't risk having read in his other, more accessible diary. Some of us are familiar with Doris Lessing's book, *The Golden Notebook*. The hero in this book, Anna, compartmentalized her life into four different journals. *The Golden Notebook* was the culmination of her inner search, a single journal that reflected all aspects of her life.

As you can see, there is no one single way to use a diary. It's best to let your own diary become what it wants to become. Think how you use or might use a diary.

Writing in a Storm or Under a Blue Sky

Many diarists are "crisis writers." Give them a crisis or conflict and they will write page after page in their notebooks. It's almost as if conflict and intense emotions fuel their desire and need to write. They write desperately in a storm, in the midst of turmoil. Perhaps for them, a journal is the eye of the hurricane, the place for reflection amidst the blowing winds and rain. Fortunately, these types of writers are able to sort out their feelings in their journals. They actually resolve conflicts through intense periods of writing. Not everyone is like this. Some diarists are "serenity writers." Give them a crisis, and writing is the last thing they do. They need peace and quiet and a relatively stable and smooth flow of life in order for them to collect themselves to write. For these writers, they prefer writing in a garden when the sky is clear and blue, and the air is fresh. This is the kind of environment in which they blossom.

Of course, the weather is always changing. The sky is not always clear and sunny, nor is it always dark and foreboding. The trick here is to identify which type of writer you tend to be. Have you noticed that your journal entries increase when you are going through a crisis, or do they decrease? If you notice a particular pattern to your writing and number of journal entries, keep it in mind. You may need to balance things a bit. If you write a lot in the storm, in crisis, try writing when you are especially happy or just loafing. If you generally write only when you are serene and relaxed, try to write about a particular emotional crisis that is blowing over your life.

No Trespassing

For many journal writers, privacy can be a critical concern. We need to feel that we're free to write anything we want in our journals. The privacy that a journal offers lets us be honest, relaxed, and uninhibited. This freedom is essential to good writing. Without it, we tend to censor our writing in fear that someone will read it. We end up hiding our journals in fear of being scolded or "found out." Some people write in shorthand or only when they're alone. This can be aggravating and dampen any desire to write.

For children journal writers, the tiny lock on a diary can offer the illusion of a privacy that seems incomparable to anything they may have experienced. To them, the lock means "No trespassing!" They may write their entries in pig latin, or in secret codes.

If you walk into any elementary school and ask a classroom of sixth graders how many of them keep journals or diaries, six or seven children will raise their hands. If you ask how many of them have read someone else's diary, you will probably see all the students waving their hands, giggling.

Students are usually quite open and frank about whose journal they read. "I read my older sister's diary" or "my mother's" or "my cousin Jim's." Most of them, however, don't recall what they read. If they do, they don't recall reading anything important. They almost look disappointed.

Most of them, lured by the possibility of discovering untold secrets, snuck into their brother's or sister's room and opened the bottom drawer of his or her desk and carefully lifted the folder under which the diary was hidden. Trembling with excitement, they had their hopes dashed when they read about his girlfriend or her boyfriend "and boring stuff like that." Many adults admit that journals hold some kind of magical attraction that makes them alluring. For this reason, it's suggested that you not leave your diaries out in the open. Sometimes clear boundaries may need to be set with spouses, housemates, even with children.

Most importantly, journals offer us solitude, not just privacy from others. The hour we take to sit down with a cup of tea or coffee and open our journals is special in a way no other hour of the day is. We are alone, facing a blank page, collecting ourselves for a moment. There may be others in the house, clanging pots and pans in the kitchen, but we are still and quiet within. We pick up our pens, glance out the window, and very carefully begin writing what we hear inside us. In this solitude, we are listening, as well as writing. This precious moment, hard to find in our busy lives, is released like a bird from its cage when we open our journals.

Children warn others not to trespass; this may mean that they are guarding something precious. Keeping your diaries out of sight ultimately protects your solitude.

Pitfalls to Journal Keeping

Many students who have taken our classes have complained, "Well, I used to keep a diary, but I haven't written in it for years." Or, "I've always wanted to keep a journal, but I just haven't been able to get started." They use the class and its weekly meetings to help structure their time to get started. Getting started is a problem for many people. One way to begin is to find a structure that will motivate you. Taking a journal writing class is one way to begin. Buy yourself a special notebook and pen. Invest your time and money somehow. Just calling a friend who keeps a diary can be motivational.

"I just don't have the time" is another common complaint of students and writers alike. "I have so many other commitments that get in the way of writing." There isn't any other way around this except to make time. Examine what you do have time for, make a list of these things, and see how many of these things are as important as your desire to start a journal. Most likely, you'll have plenty of things, like washing dishes, house cleaning, mowing the lawn, cleaning the basement, that in your mind are not as important, yet are necessary. Still, if you put a value on these things, journal writing may win out.

Avoid making pledges and signing statements that you'll write two or three hours per day. If you write one page each day, you'll be doing very well. Keep it simple! Most professional writers would be overjoyed to write a page a day. We feel this would be an accomplishment and a balance to our erratic writing schedules which sometimes involve writing three to four hours daily, then long stretches, even months, of very little writing. Instead of promising to write so many hours daily, think of a schedule that will help you to write *more regularly*.

"I don't have any of these problems. I write a lot and quite regularly. It's just that what I write seems, well, dumb or meaningless," said one student. Another student made a similar remark. "It seems I'm making the same entry in my journal every day." This is often heard in workshops. Be careful of judging your own writing. Often, we're not discerning when it comes to our own writing. We put ourselves down too much.

You'd be amazed how weak writing can become exciting writing with a few strokes of an editor's pen. What actually may be interfering is something personal and has nothing to do with the quality of the work. In writing workshops, there will always be students who feel their work is inferior to everyone else's. Often, these students' writings show remarkable vitality.

On the opposite end of this negative evaluation is the thought that you are writing a masterpiece, a literary coup d'état. Only later, do you plummet out of those joyous heights down to earth, realizing the many flaws.

If you're troubled with the question of how good or bad your writing is, how interesting or dull it is, put the question aside and concentrate on writing the truth, what you really feel and think. Write clearly without disguising what you say by carefully selecting words. Though it's not unusual to hear people admit that they've written lies in their journals, the truth will serve you better. Tell it straight out! Here's what Brenda Ueland says in her marvelous book, *If You Want To Write.*

...write...a true, careless, slovenly, impulsive, honest
diary every day of your life....You must in time learn
to write from your true self...in your letters and diary.
— Brenda Ueland

"My problem is none of these things," one student remarked.
"I write regularly, and have for years. I enjoy it very much.
I set aside time each day, or almost each day, to write. It's just
that I don't know what to do with it all. I mean I have over ten
notebooks for this year alone. I'd like to do something with it."
If this is your problem, you should find in this book a variety
of writing forms into which you can structure your work more
formally. Another book, full of helpful ideas, is Tristine Rainer's
The New Diary.

The most persistent and fundamental problem for most
writers is, as Woody Allen says, "showing up at the ball park."
Getting to your desk and opening the journal resolves 90 percent of the problems you'll ever face. If you can do this regularly, you've got the basic problem licked.

Writing about Secrets

An often quoted saying is: "You are only as sick as your
secrets." Secrets are often associated with shame. They become experiences we can not tell anyone. The worst kinds
of secrets are the ones we keep to ourselves, telling no one,
not even therapists. These secrets are deadly and whittle
away our self-esteem. The following exercise will aid you
by unearthing those experiences buried inside and kept secret
for years.

First, write three secrets in your journal using only a few
words that will sufficiently summon the experience to your
mind. These three secrets should be experiences that you have
kept secret from others and have never told anyone. If you are
fortunate to have no such secrets, and in fact have confided
these experiences to a therapist, counselor, or close friend, then

list three experiences that used to be secrets. They should be about what you would not easily share. After you've done this, set them aside for a short time. Think about them.

Second, select one particular secret to work with. It should be the one that seems most unresolved to you, the worst secret, the most intense in your memory.

Allow yourself the option of throwing this exercise away after it's completed. It's important that you feel free to write openly and uninhibitedly. Muster up your courage. You might write this on separate paper from your diary.

Third, write as quickly as you can and jot down a list of details that come to your mind about this secret. For example, you might jot down nouns and verbs like elm tree, sidewalk, evening, moonlight, a curl, a belt, walking, sashaying, pitching a stone, a crash. Whatever you write, push yourself into exhausting every detail. After you have done this, put your list aside and take a break.

Fourth, now write in narrative the entire episode. Be sure not to flinch and shy away from writing it in its entirety. If you stop in the middle and don't know what to write next, look back at your list of details, and choose one to expand on.

This exercise can be quite thrilling after it's done. Unburdening yourself of the secrets and shame through writing can free you to write more openly about other experiences. It will energize you. You can assume that since you've written about your darkest secrets there isn't anything you can't write about. Every subject in the world is available to you. You no longer are kept by shame from writing about any topic you choose.

Journals and the Twelve Steps

Journals and diaries are excellent tools for a First Step because the diary is private, and individuals may feel more secure about writing their secrets, their powerlessness. As the First Step reads:

We admitted we were powerless over alcohol — that our lives had become unmanageable.

For example, we've included an excerpt here from a journal written by Terry T., an Al-Anon member. While sitting by a river, he becomes painfully conscious of how his spouse's gambling affects him. He wrote this entry years before he attended Al-Anon meetings and could openly discuss the problem. Only now, after reading past journals, does he realize how his secret was carefully being told in his diaries long before he realized it.

All the money is gone. I sat down by the river today and watched the boat wakes roll toward the banks and thought, "The bank's not empty just empty of me, it's a hole I have to fill." I wondered if that emptiness would keep me afloat. The sky was full of those white clouds that look like smoke signals, row after row of them, as though the sky were a farmer's field. The water leaden, the color of garbage cans. Now the sky is the same color and it's raining. Water always seems to know when company's coming. I threw stones out into the water, dozens of them, one after another, until my shoulder ached. I can't fill the river with stones. I can throw my anger at the current and it's swept away in a quick splash. I can't blame myself for that either. The money seems so far away now. It was real. The reality now is I hurt. The minute facts are this: my throat aches with the same grief I felt as a child when my new Davy Crockett rifle disappeared. It was part of my identity. I was Dave Crockett in the back yard, in the shrubs of neighbors, on the dirt piles next to the dug out basements of the postwar building boom. Now part of my self is gone again. But here I am. No money. No rifle. Just me again. It's raining. I'm empty. No, I'm not empty. I have pain, hands to throw rocks, eyes to cry with.
— Terry T.

For a Fourth Step inventory diaries may seem to be less intimidating than a formal Fourth Step guidebook. The Fourth Step says:

Made a searching and fearless moral inventory of ourselves.

Writing "a searching and fearless moral inventory" may give the individual a chance to reflect and remember experiences that otherwise might not have been recalled. In addition, the journal can be an excellent place to continue working our inventory as stated in the Tenth Step:

Continued to take personal inventory and when we were wrong promptly admitted it.

Writing about Our Spirituality

Journals offer writers the chance to explore and make more clear their own understanding of their Higher Power. The idea of a Higher Power is first mentioned in the Second Step, which says:

Came to believe that a Power greater than ourselves could restore us to sanity.

This focus on spirituality continues in the Third Step, which states:

Made a decision to turn our will and our lives over to the care of God *as we understood Him.*

Through writing, you can deepen your ideas and feelings about God, "as we understand Him." But the word *Him* with its connotations of gender is a stumbling block for some people when they begin their spiritual work. Some people in the program prefer to say the Step in this way:

Made a decision to turn our will and our lives over to the care of God *as we understand God.*

The writer Rachel V. has written about her coming to terms with the Steps:

> Because of the difficulties I have had with the description of God as exclusively male, I have crossed out the *Him's* and *He's* in the Steps...and inserted the word God so that there is no reference to God being one sex or another....That way my God can be a female Buddha or Jesus Christ if I want; or an Inner Light, like the Quakers describe....Not having such a concept tied to sex reminds me that the power I am attempting to describe is without limit.
>
> — Rachel V.

Rachel V. is writing about her understanding. Writing *brings* understanding.

Once you engage the process of writing, communicating with your deeper self, new spiritual understanding develops. At first, the very notion of God or Higher Power can be vague and abstract. However, getting it down on paper makes your thoughts and feelings more credible and clearer.

In our minds, thoughts don't often challenge us to be specific and clear. On the other hand, writing, the very act of picking up a pencil, pressing our thumbs near the point, and setting it down on a blank piece of paper challenges us to be clear, precise, and specific. Our thoughts leap around and away from the subject, but our pencils slow them down, make them more accountable.

You can address God or your Higher Power in your journal the same way some people address their journals by starting with "Dear Diary." You can explore your own spirituality this way. You needn't write, "Dear God," but don't be embarrassed to do so if that helps you get started. The point is to keep your

Higher Power always in mind as you write. One student, in her mid-thirties, keeps a diary and still begins each entry with "Dear God." You might recall that Alice Walker's book, *The Color Purple,* is structured this way. Summoning a presence or power to aid us in performing a particular rite like writing or art is found in many cultures. Use this device if it helps.

Begin your entry by writing a brief description of yourself as a child involved in some specific religious ritual, like saying your prayers in your pajamas at your bedside. Do you recall asking God to take care of your parents, maybe even helping you with a math test the next day? Perhaps you remember being an altar boy, kneeling at the foot of the altar in your black cassock and white surplice, repeating prayers in Latin. Describe this scene.

Be sure to be as specific as you can. Write as many details of your memory as possible. Imagine yourself kneeling at your bedside. Is there a carpet? Or is the floor bare? Do your knees hurt? Is your mother or father in the room with you? Is the bed made? Are you in a hurry to finish your prayers? Or, are you especially devout, lowering your head, folding your hands?

After you've done this, write a short evaluation of your spirituality at that time. How do you regard this child that you were? Immature? Childish? Or sincere and searching? Evaluate the good and the bad, the ignorance and the wisdom, the simplicity and the convoluted. What aspects of your religious life, as childish as it may have been, do you still admire in the picture you described? What aspects give you negative feelings, if any? How have you grown spiritually?

Next, write a description of yourself involved in some religious or spiritual practice today. You could be attending church, a temple, or an Alcoholics Anonymous (AA) meeting. You could be meditating, practicing transcendental meditation, giving a massage, or praying. Repeat the same process, describing the scene in detail and then asking yourself the same questions you asked yourself about the childhood scene. How do you regard this adult that you are? Immature? Childish? Vulnerable or acquiescent? Wise?

You can seek to deepen your spiritual life through means such as writing. Your journal can help you to sort things out, reflect and meditate, and clarify your spiritual values.

CHAPTER 2

Automatic Pilot: Stream of Consciousness

Rest on the flow of effort.
— Danin Katagiri

Speed writing or rush writing is also called *stream of consciousness* writing. It is simply writing without stopping, without thinking about what's being written. Speed writing is like putting an airplane on automatic pilot. For this reason, we identify stream of consciousness writing by calling it *automatic pilot.* We switch over our controls or give them up to allow a deeper self to drive or direct us as we write. We free-associate. Impulse is allowed to pilot us as we write. We disregard punctuation, spelling, grammar, and the logical order of language for that other voice in us that rambles willy-nilly of any grammatical rules. That voice may skip around from past to present, reality to fantasy, mumble and mutter all day long; it's a voice often stifled, a dream-like voice, uncensored and uninhibited, a wise and playful voice.

The stream of consciousness is not a stream in a particular person, but rather a stream we all share in. You only need to step in and be a part of it. Let the syllables, the words, and the sentences form themselves, whether they abide by grammatical rules or not. It may feel awkward at first, but if you persist you'll find yourself enjoying these moments of writing. In fact, it won't be long before you remark to yourself, *That's really good writing. I'm impressed!* At first, it may feel as if someone else has written it. In time, though, you'll learn how to tap into those resources and flow more and more.

Here's a brief example of automatic piloting.

> words are numbered balls tossed in a large hoop and spun to play bingo and this is how unpredictable my life was and I was unpredictable and each hour was a word a numbered ball and I wanted to stand up and shout bingo and have my life run smooth and success-fully but every hour turned up on someone else's card while I sat on a chair of self-pity and only a drink would help me until I finally said I hate playing games and I'm going home and who cares anyhow but I did and the large hoop kept spinning and spinning uncon-trollably.

Notice that the writer never bothered to punctuate the writing. We can feel how the writer was swept up in the flow of words.

Your Own Style

If you actually record what this inner voice says verbatim, you'll discover that this voice has a way of being correct and natural on paper even though it may violate standard gram-matical rules. That voice may be called your personal writing style. As each individual has a characteristic manner of talk-ing, so does each individual have a similar manner of writ-ing. Try not to struggle to write a perfect, grammatical sentence, but write in a way that reflects your unique and individual per-sonality. Write like you talk, for starters.

Writing style is very much like personality. Many people can quickly identify writers of particular stories or poems by the writing style. Think of well-known writers you've read, and immediately their writing style comes to mind. You may think of the long, flowing sentences of Henry James, the lush details of Proust, the somber and dry Dostoevsky, the sensuousness of Anaïs Nin, the spiritual complexity of characters in Flannery O'Connor. These writers show a personality on paper.

Stream of consciousness is a writing technique especially helpful for writers to discover and develop their own style. There is no one quite like you. When writing, let it show.

You will find Peter Elbow's book, *Writing Without Teachers*, an excellent source in learning to write more freely and spontaneously, as well as how to adapt stream of consciousness to other kinds of writing.

The Flow of Words

The purpose of this next exercise is to have you write nonstop for a short time without any consideration of grammatical rules, punctuation, syntax, or thematic development.

We suggest you begin with short periods of automatic writing by timing yourself. Get a clock or set your watch alongside your notebook, typewriter, or computer. If your watch has an alarm, set it for five to ten minutes. Keep your pens or pencils moving across the page. Keep your fingers dancing over the keyboard. Keep your hand flowing across the paper, like a wave that rolls across the water. Don't hesitate or stop; pause only to cross your t's or dot your i's. If you should find yourself hesitating, looking out your window and nibbling on the pencil's eraser, wondering what you should write, stop and get back to writing. Even if all you write is repetitive phrases. Anything! Just as long as you keep writing.

If you find yourself stuck, without a thought, feeling, or sensation, you might write (just to keep the flow uninterrupted) about this directly, as the writer did below.

> I can't think of a thing to write, my mind is a complete
> blank blank as the white as the white clouds only there
> isn't anything going to rain and since my mind is this
> way and my heart is going the other way and I am in

between with nothing to write to say to shout to whisper to cry to hum where then am I am I even here in this chair and who is writing and pushing my hand across this paper.

The above writing has that characteristic flow of stream of consciousness with its run-on sentences, lack of punctuation, and repetition. This kind of writing may not appeal to you. In fact, punctuation may be automatically and naturally included. But, when you find yourself straining, unsure whether to use a period or semi-colon, then it's time to forget it and keep on writing. Just keep your pen moving, and sooner or later you will discover your voice, a natural ordering of words on the page that reflects your manner of talking. Again, time yourself. Write without interruption. Don't think about what you are going to write; let your pen do the thinking. Think and feel on the paper, not in your head.

Here's a simple example of writing that shows that spontaneous quality of writing which indicates stream of consciousness. This piece was written by Donna Howard Husby, showing how rush writing can be focused on a single topic. It's called "Stream Of Tears."

I cry all the time. No, that's not true not all the time and probably not even most of the time though it seems like it because I cry more than anybody else I know if in fact we ever know how much other people cry because they don't do it in public places like I do although at least some of them do some of the time because you see them in movies or airports but that's acceptable and they cry acceptably I mean one or two tears which trickle gracefully down the cheek wouldn't count as crying if I wrote the manual which I almost have and would like to sponsor a contest too for the most prolific tear duct the loudest choking and sobbing the reddest face the most nasal dripping etc. because I'd win them all. I mean when I cry I really cry and my parents should have invested in tissue stock because they'd be rich by now which would be making the best of a very bad thing for them....

— Donna Howard Husby

This writing is light, humorous, and a good example of letting go of the controls or logic of language and letting words flow from the right side of our brains.

In this next example, poet Phebe Hanson writes out of a flow that is more inclusive and rich in detail.

Here I am on the North Shore of Lake Superior, Tofte, Minnesota, at this time in December, with two women friends, on a three-day spiritual retreat, fully-planned back in Minneapolis to include at least 24 hours of fasting, modified at the last minute by our decision to allow ourselves liquids, so we pack the car with juices, cranberry-raspberry, pineapple-coconut, apple, carrot, and orange, lemon-flavored mineral water, chamomile, anise, and sleepytime teas and we've agreed also to at least three hours of silence each day and before the first period, we ready ourselves by listening to a cassette tape meditation exercise led by Shakti Gawain, whose book on creative visualization I've read before I came and whom I'd creatively visualized as from some exotic country such as India or Tibet, but who turns out to sound on the tape heartily Scandinavian-Midwestern, someone you'd never be afraid to let talk you into a creative visualization, so firmly grounded does her voice seem in down-to-earth matter of factness. We all sit straight-backed in chairs facing the picture window that looks out on Lake Superior....Of course, I'm not thinking all this during the visualization because Shakti keeps me pretty busy making images, and now she's telling me to surround my image with a pink bubble, because pink is the color associated with the heart, and it will bring you that which is in perfect affinity with your being, so underneath that pink bubble on the white fur rug....

— Phebe Hanson

Phebe Hanson's writing is generous and rich. She's included countless detail and information. Try using any of the last three examples as models for your own writing. You can write about writing as you read in the first example, about one particular subject as in "Stream of Tears," or you can write a piece that is as inclusive and rich in detail as Phebe Hanson's.

Natalie Goldberg's book, *Writing Down The Bones*, sheds light on this subject of "automatic piloting" and offers specific writing exercises that will help you to break from more logical and rational approaches to writing. Appropriately subtitled, *Freeing The Writer Within*, Goldberg uses her own background in Zen meditation to encourage writers to let the inner voice speak without inhibition or censoring.

If you practice these short, timed five-to-ten minute writing sessions, you will soon discover how easy and natural it is to let your pen flow across the paper. You will have fewer inhibitions, fewer moments of panic or paralysis when facing the blank page. Moving your pen across the paper (or your fingers over the keyboard) will be as easy as starting up your car engine. No more than ten of these timed writing exercises will have your pen purring and the inner motor revving, ready to let your true voice and style flow naturally down those thin roads on lined paper. You may find yourself leaping from one subject to the next; you may find yourself writing about a single subject, as if in a tunnel burrowing deeper and deeper.

One final word about this particular stream of consciousness writing: let it be fun! You may already know many writing instructors who suggest this free-flowing writing technique, and most of them will encourage a playful attitude.

If you think of rush writing as a roller coaster instead of a stream or airplane, you may find this exercise more enjoyable, as well as more instructive. Besides, this may help change this carnival ride to a more positive image, opposed to the negative one that comes from years of wanting to "get off the roller coaster." If the image of a roller coaster suits you, then we challenge you to ride it with "no hands." Some adventurous people on roller coasters will "show off" by raising their hands high above their heads when the roller coaster chugs up a steep hill, and at the very top these people will wave their hands frantically, shouting as the ride plummets down. In this same spirit, set your watches or clocks for ten minutes, and ride on your roller coaster "no hands." Show off!

After you've practiced this exercise, see if you can come up with your own name for the exercise. We've already suggested images of airplanes, streams, rivers, cars, and roller coasters. What other images can you think of? Come up with one that suits you the best, one that lets you get into it.

Warm-Ups

The purpose of automatic pilot or stream of consciousness writing is twofold: first, this technique will help you to acquire your own writing style. Second, this exercise will loosen you up for other writing.

Aerobic exercise, or for that matter any kind of physical exercise, requires warm-ups. We stretch muscles, loosen them up. We even do this with cars in winter. We let them idle and warm before we drive them. In a similar way, stream of consciousness lets us warm up. It blows out the cobwebs in our minds, heats up our feelings, and kindles our desire. At the same time, it relaxes our inner censors, lets us lower our guard, and write more naturally.

Below, we will discuss where, when, and how you write as ways of preparing, warming up, and relaxing to let yourself flow more easily in the stream of words and consciousness.

Where You Write

Besides automatic writing, there are other warm-up exercises and techniques you can practice and use. For instance, writing in unfamiliar locations, such as cafes or restaurants, waiting rooms in doctor's offices, in offices, in bed, even in different rooms of your house or apartment. Changing the place where you write can affect your writing in the same way as automatic or rush writing. In unusual locations, you may find yourself writing quickly and without inhibition. Sitting in a doctor's office may only give you ten minutes to write, the same ten minutes you've already learned how to use in your stream of consciousness writing. If you ride a bus to work, a bumpy ride might be just the thing for your thick, felt pen to write spontaneously. A place like a library may add a more reflective quality to your writing. At a restaurant, surrounded by strangers, you may find yourself able to write more directly and simply, with less anxiety. Of course, public writing may have the opposite affect. The idea is to explore different locations as a way of loosening yourself up so that you might write more naturally and in your own style.

One writer keeps a yellow note pad on the front seat of her car alongside her whenever she drives long distances. Although this could be dangerous, the situation requires her to jot a few notes quickly and without delay. In this way, she makes use of stream of consciousness writing.

To demonstrate how place may affect your writing, we think of a particular student who found herself stuck and unable to write. At night, after her children were asleep and her husband was watching a favorite late night television program, she would retire to the bedroom and, while in bed with her notebook propped up on her legs, she would try to write. She complained of being stuck and inhibited. She just couldn't get her pen moving, or if she did, she didn't enjoy what she wrote. "I used to love writing for an hour or so before bedtime. I just can't figure out what happened," she complained.

After talking at length about this, the student discovered that writing was most fun and exciting for her when she was sitting in a particular rocking chair that once had been in the bedroom. The chair had been moved out into the living room, and she tried writing in bed. Although many people find writing in bed an ideal place, this particular person did not. Finally, she got the rocking chair back and, to her delight, she discovered that this in fact was the core of the problem. Within a short time, she was writing every night, as usual, before bedtime. In this case, a change of location did not help, but a change from bed to the rocking chair did.

Experiment with writing in various places before you decide on one that works best. And if you already prefer writing in a certain room, we still urge you to observe how writing in another room in your house might affect your writing.

Here's another practice that might help you warm up and prepare for longer writing exercises. For one week carry a small note pad with you and jot down phrases, sensations, snatches of memories, quotes, colors, the names of flowers or cars, slogans from billboards you pass on the highway, the names of streets that interest you for some particular reason, words that might describe the shapes of noses or mouths, a word you find appealing because of its sensuousness, the style of someone's suit or dress, odd gestures or facial expression. Jot down all the bits and pieces that leave imprints on your thoughts. Gather these impressions together. Later on you might use these impressions for more lengthy writing. You may not. They may stay in the notebook as simple impressions or exercises that keep you limber and alert throughout the day.

When You Write

When, as well as where, you write may also greatly affect your writing. Many seasoned writers prefer to write in the mornings, while some prefer the evenings. Some writers will spend hours writing late in the evening, only to find themselves years later writing in the morning. The time you choose to write may vary from year to year and depend on such things as employment, children, vacations, even grants.

If you have a young infant, try to take advantage of the child's nap time and write for a short time during it. One writer holding down a job at a hospital wrote in his diary during coffee breaks. You might cut out reading the Sunday morning paper, take one night a week to write at the library, or spend one hour each Saturday morning at a coffee shop.

We also suggest you read Dorthea Brande's *Becoming A Writer.* In her book, you'll find a lengthy warm-up exercise you can do upon the first few minutes of awakening, when your eyes are still filled with dreams. This book may be especially helpful for readers who like to work with dreams and write in that half-awake and half-asleep state.

There is an endearing anecdote that addresses this subject of making time to write. A nationally known poet named William Stafford had decided to rise and write an hour before everyone in his family woke up. He woke each morning at 5:30 A.M. to enjoy writing during this quiet hour before his children awoke and the normal clash of silverware at the breakfast table began. One of his daughters, however, who must have heard her father bustling about one morning, awoke. She was delighted to have her father's undivided attention. Subsequently, she, too, got up an hour before everyone else in order to spend the time with him. As William Stafford tells the story, he had to rise another hour earlier, at 4:30 A.M., in order to be alone to write.

Stafford's story is the answer to people who can't find the time to write in their busy lives. This answer makes us bite the bullet. We have to make time. And we will, for those of us who really need to write. It will be a test of your ingenuity to somehow eke out a few minutes each day to write.

If you want to write, if you want to use writing as a way of exploring your personal growth, if you want to use stream of consciousness to discover and strengthen your own writing style, if you think writing is a way to heal wounds and reach into your whole self, then take time to do it. Think of this writing more as a necessity than a luxury. Many people consider their morning walk as something that keeps them healthy, so they continually make time to do it. Writing can be the same for you.

The expression "made a decision" echoes throughout the Twelve Step programs. Make a decision now to put aside some time to write. What is most important is that you keep a consistent schedule. The discipline people talk about in order to write consists primarily in writing regularly, not necessarily for great lengths of time. It's like anything else you do. Playing the piano, jogging, reading, shooting pool, swimming, or even bowling require practice and effort to keep the activity in your life.

Even if you write every other day for fifteen minutes and keep to this schedule, you're doing very well. Possibly, you might set aside fifteen minutes for related writing activities, such as reading, cleaning off your desk top, going out to buy a new notebook or pen, finishing a few letters, or rummaging through old journals. Taking a little time like this each day lets you prepare, keep warmed-up, and be ready.

What You Write With

This may seem like we are belaboring the point. But, until you find out exactly the type of pen you like to write with, the kind of notebook, and whether you prefer typewriters to computers, give some thought to the subject of supplies. Besides, it's fun to include a discussion of your favorite pen or paper as a part of the ritual of writing, of warming-up, and getting into that flow or stream of consciousness.

Let Others Inspire You

We remind you once again that stream of consciousness has a two-fold purpose. It helps you

• Discover your writing style, and
• Loosen up to write later at length

Of course, there are other benefits to automatic writing, but for now we are concentrating on these two and finding ways in this chapter to further develop these exercises.

Another exercise involves letting other writers, poets, journalists, essayists, or diarists inspire your own quick writing. Go to the library and try to locate the journals and workbooks of one writer you admire. Often, in these books a writer's work is less polished and more spontaneous. They are invaluable aids that hopefully encourage you to do similar work and writing. Many writers use journals to record ideas they'll write about later, or they'll use them to keep themselves in the flow of writing, with their engines always warmed-up and revving.

If you can't think of any writer to research, we suggest you read the journals of Anaïs Nin, Virginia Woolf, Andre Gide, or Fyodor Dostoevsky.

You'll see how Anaïs Nin records one lush, sensuous image after another, never hesitating, almost as if there's a detective in each sentence revealing each detailed image or impression. See how she applies this technique when she's writing about her circle of friends. Her stream of consciousness is exotic, personal, and inviting.

Note how Virginia Woolf's writing resembles a river flowing endlessly from sentence to sentence, never really interrupting itself, flowing out of some great oceanic inner source.

Gide, too, writes long sentences that would leave most of us breathless. His journals seem to be written without any self-consciousness. He puts all his life into them.

On the other hand, Dostoevsky's workbooks reveal the novelist jotting ideas and elaborating on characters. His maplike notes and sentences appear complex, with a single purpose. He does not struggle in his workbook to write perfect sentences or descriptions.

Half the trick of writing is letting others motivate and spur you on. Hopefully, their writing will be more a cause for inspiration than envy.

More Writing Exercises for Your Automatic Pilot

Stream of consciousness writing will often allow past

experiences to surface that might otherwise be left submerged in our unconscious mind. Spontaneous writing, like psychoanalytical free-association, releases memories that are normally censored. In this way, automatic or rush writing can be utilized to reawaken memories and past experiences.

The following exercise may help you rediscover episodes in your life. Again, give yourself approximately ten minutes. Instead of writing willy-nilly about anything, however, you must channel the energy from spontaneous writing and direct it toward a certain subject.

Before you begin writing, select a general subject you want to write about. The subject could be divorce, losing a job, anorexia, incest, alcoholism, or more joyful subjects such as marriage, the birth of your child, a sobriety anniversary, or getting a new job.

You might select the subject of family illness. Perhaps one of your family members had suffered or died from a fatal, chronic illness. It may have been alcoholism. Or cancer. You may have a child with spina bifida.

We've included an example of a student's to show you how varied stream of consciousness is. His name is Peter Fleck, and he chose to write about his child's birth.

> She called me up at work, I remember. *My water broke* is a wave crashing to the floor in the bathroom. *Don't rush, take the bus, there's plenty of time.* We stayed up all night waiting for your arrival   your mother like a whale slowly turning in the dim light   swimming deeper   alone with you her cries heralding you. I remember stars   outside when I would have a cigarette   alone   with the dark night hoping you would get here okay   unsure what to do. Two hours after sunrise your hair slick like black metal appeared between her legs and you slid down the birth canal tiny and wrinkled   into my hands.
>
> — Peter Fleck

In this example, the student used spacing throughout his writing. The spaces indicate pauses, hesitations, or reflection. Try writing similarly about a particular topic. Select one that has fairly strong emotion, as Peter Fleck did. Set your clock or watch for approximately ten minutes and write as quickly as possible about the subject. Let yourself be swept up by the flow of words. You'll know it when it happens. It may remind you of running, ice-skating, something swift. Let sensations — smells, sounds, sights, tastes, and touches — come up in your memory. Do not stop writing until the time is up.

Automatic Pilot and Self-Discovery

If you have a nagging problem at work and sense something is wrong but you can't put your finger on it, automatic pilot writing can be very helpful. Focus on one particular problem. Ask yourself, *What am I doing to sabotage my job (or relationship, et cetera)?* Then write nonstop on the subject until some new information appears. You don't always have to set a clock. Instead, you could write nonstop for a certain length or number of pages. Writing automatically until two pages are filled can be just as effective as writing for ten minutes.

Piloting through the Twelve Steps

Stream of consciousness writing itself is unmanaged by the writer. We've seen how it may allow unpredictable memories or feelings to surface. This kind of writing lends itself to all the Steps, especially Step One. Rush writing itself creates a sense of powerlessness. You do not direct, control, or manage the flow of words.

Stream of consciousness can be applied to all the Steps as a way to get your feelings and thoughts out, like a rough draft. Write quickly and naturally. Free associate from one memory to another. For the Fourth Step, write an inventory of a particular feeling, say anger. Write nonstop until you have exhausted the subject.

Anger is not a flame burning or a pot with a lid or a bottle of pop frozen and minutes away from shattering but anger is I mean my anger is always so far away like a fluttering of dark wings on the horizon or my anger lies down in a pile of rags in a hot attic room and sometimes my anger is an unloaded gun in a drawer and I know how far away I am from anger and how far the two of us anger and I must travel until we integrate and anger becomes a spontaneous expression that is not aimed at anyone. I remember when I yelled at my son for leaving a hammer and pliers outside for two days. It rained and the tools began to rust and my anger got corked inside a bottle until a week later when my son asked for a tool and the cork shot out from the carbonation of anger shaking inside me all that time.

For the Eighth Step list the people you've harmed. The Eighth Step says:

Made a list of all persons we had harmed, and became willing to make amends to them all.

Start with one person. As soon as another comes to mind, leave the first individual and write extensively about the second individual until a third person pops into your mind. Don't try to keep track of it all. Just write until you feel you are caught in a flow of words and language.

I started fifteen years ago stealing a bottle of wine from the cellar of a professor at the University of Montana a kind man helpful and I stole this red wine hiding it under my shirt like I did one time long ago in Chicago where I worked for a beer distributor and stole some money from the till not much I have to say but I stole and I even remember the delicatessen store way back when I was twelve and I stole a magazine or a candy bar and if I remember I stole a dime or a quarter from my dad's change lying on the kitchen table once and all this sounds trivial but each theft of small amounts say a quarter was magnified by guilt and shame into a hundred quarters.

This same exercise can be applied to your Higher Power. Apply it to your work on Step Two and Step Three. Apply it to Step Eleven:

Sought through prayer and meditation to improve our conscious contact with God *as we understood Him,* praying only for knowledge of His will for us and the power to carry that out.

Although you'll find other exercises in this book related to understanding your Higher Power, you can begin now by simply writing, free-associating, about what your Higher Power is. You might begin with simply writing: *"My Higher Power is. . ."* You may repeat this over and over until ideas, thoughts, or feelings begin to pour out from your pen. The line itself may change to: *"My Higher Power is not. . ."*

A Jump over the Rough Spots

Finally, we'd like to suggest you use this writing technique throughout this book as a way of jumping over the rough spots you encounter in writing. Whenever you find yourself resistant, blocked, without ideas, your mind blank, try using this technique to jump over the obstacle. Put aside the paper or poem or story you were working on and write spontaneously on the subject that seems to block you. Write around the subject, come through its back door by writing obliquely about it until you find that rush of current that will release whatever is pent up.

Rush writing is used by all kinds of writers. You can use it as a means of discovering what you want to write in essays; in poems, it can be used to pursue a particular image that eludes you; in stories, it can create more generous descriptions; when making lists, it can spawn new sensations or ideas or details. The more you use this technique, the more easily you will be able to immerse yourself into that inner river of spontaneous expression.

CHAPTER 3

"Just the Facts, Ma'am": Descriptive Writing

No ideas, but in things.
— William Carlos Williams

The phrase, "Just the facts, Ma'am," comes from an old television series called *Dragnet*. The star in *Dragnet*, Jack Webb, played Sergeant Joe Friday and was always in hot pursuit of the *facts*, the details. A witness might relate to Jack Webb why a particular person was robbed or murdered, but he always interrupted and reminded the person that he was only interested in the facts, "just the facts." Jack could draw his conclusions and find a motive for the crime later, but he first needed the facts.

Writing facts and details are crucial. We often overlook details when writing and fall into speculation, telling, abstracting, and reasoning. Not that these things are bad, but without details these processes alone are ineffective. Although the quality of your writing may not be critically important to you, your writing will improve immensely when concrete details are recorded.

The Difference between Showing and Telling

Feelings and thoughts are best expressed when writers show their emotions and ideas. *Show, don't tell* is a phrase often quoted by writing instructors. There is a significant difference

37

between these two words, *show* and *tell*. This chapter will make the difference clear.

A telling statement might be, "I think she is worried about something." This statement tells us something about someone, whom we only know to be a woman, and that she is worried. The statement does not show us anything. You do not see her upset. If the person rewrites the sentence, "Linda's eyes are red, her hands are shaking. She whispers, 'It's time for me to pack,' " then we can visualize what the writer is talking about. We get a picture of Linda and can easily conclude that she is indeed upset and about to leave for somewhere.

If the writer gives us the facts, in this case the red eyes, the shaking hands, the whispered remark, we, like Jack Webb, can draw our conclusions. Whenever you write, try to include the details, to create a picture.

Brenda Ueland stresses in her book the importance of *seeing* what you are writing. When advising students whose stories lack a certain spark, she says:

> Do not try to think of better *words*. . . . Try to see the people better. See them — just what they did and how they looked and felt. Then write it.
>
> — Brenda Ueland

Our senses give us facts and help to create an environment. They make the reality of our own experiences and memories more tangible. You'll find various exercises in this chapter to encourage you to write what you see, smell, taste, touch, and hear.

You might say, "But there aren't any words to describe what happened." Your experience may seem ineffable. But the fact is that this is just what writers do. They find words to describe in a fresh manner experiences whose magic often gets lost in everyday speech. The facts and details are so important to writing that we've placed this chapter early in the book so you might be able to apply what you learn here to the other chapters and writing exercises.

For a simple warm-up exercise, try rewriting the following sentences that tell more than they show, as we did earlier with the sentence, "I think she is worried about something." Take a sheet of paper and show and describe what the sentences below fail to do.

- She feels hurt and wants to leave the party.
- He seems frightened.
- She is in a hurry.
- He appears to be embarrassed.
- His neighbor is very angry and does not want to talk.

Start by Writing What You See Outside Your Window

Many writers choose to write at a desk or table placed near a window. Looking outside your window might be a pleasant distraction when you find yourself stuck in your writing and lost for words. Or it can be a relaxing way to begin your writing. In either case, this section will encourage you to look outside and carefully note what you see, smell, or hear. You could be sipping coffee or tea as you gaze out. Take time to look out now because you will be asked to write a detailed description of what you see.

Here are some questions that you might find pertinent as you look out your window.

- Are your neighbor's drapes half-closed, the storm window left partially open, a shovel wedged in a mound of snow? Do boot tracks lead to the back door?
- What kind of birds do you see or hear?
- What color is the sky?

    Carefully observe the smallest details as a detective might.

- Are there shadows of branches towering over your neighbor's house that make figures on the roof?
- Is there a casement window on the third floor open?

Again, be a detective and search for these facts and make observations that involve your senses.

Here is an example of a simple description of what one man in Al-Anon saw outside his kitchen window:

> I'm sitting at my kitchen window looking outside. My neighbor's back screen door slams back and forth as the hot summer wind blows, then hushes, then blows again. The garage door is open and her car is gone. She's probably out shopping. A thin layer of dust shades the driveway. The gutter, broken from its brace, sags. It feels threatening. Anyone might walk under it just when it snaps and be speared. I rub my eyes. Just a week ago, I watched my son from this very kitchen window, chasing a black and white calico cat in their back yard. That afternoon my son was wearing a new blue shirt his grandmother bought him on his birthday a month ago. And now, as I sit quietly with my hand under my chin, it hurts to note his absence, the dust, the broken gutter, the slamming screen door. It will be weeks before I see him again.

The author is successful in his short description because he uses simple, active verbs like *slams, hushes* that have sounds. He uses verbs that are visual like *sags, shades,* and verbs you can almost feel like *rub, speared.* His nouns are equally strong and direct. By carefully selecting his details, he creates an intense, melancholic mood. By simply mentioning the absence of one particular detail — his son — the author deepens the meaning of his observations. Not once does the author *tell* you, "I'm lonely," or "I miss my son." Yet you know these things because he *shows* you his feelings.

Here's another example written by the poet and writer John Minczeski. He writes about his garden as he sits in his backyard.

Evening cool. Sitting in the back yard. Green grass, blue sky, the rhododendrons past blooming. New growth has replaced their purple blossoms. They're like crepe paper when they're crammed inside their buds. When they bloom they're like helicopters carrying us away. The blossoms don't really look like rotors until they pop off their stems and lay on the ground, purple as Caesar's robe, but with thick rotors that could spin you right up. But they're gone now. . . . it's tempered with a blooming of lilacs, honeysuckle and chokecherry, those woody, green scent-factories that border our small city lot. The Virginia Blue Bells are tolling and the violets are far from being violated. For purple, a few violas are peeping out behind some phlox in an area I haven't gotten around to weeding yet. . . . As secret as this garden is, shielded on both sides by two neighbors and an enormous garage. . . . Just a few neighbors who stand at their fence and ask what something is — like the Japanese tree lilac when it blooms around Memorial day and into June. . . .

— John Minczeski

Notice how lush and detailed his writing is. He involves our senses. We can nearly smell the lilacs blooming, almost hear the Virginia Blue Bells tolling. Minczeski uses the same writing technique in the excerpt below which is about the homeless. He simply writes the details of his observations.

You see them everywhere these days. Tonight, outside the Town Square parking lot, a guy was picking up his shopping bags he had sewn out of canvas. It looked like custom jobs, and he started ambling off again. Three bags, like anchors holding him to this earth. There was the usual grey overcoat that hung down mid-calf, the rubber overshoes though it was not slushy anymore. He picked up his bags and started moving off, slowly, limping first with one foot, then with the next.

He was like a slow-moving ship moving crosswise in
rough seas, like a tugboat pushing ahead. A round
body and a face that must have been fifty or sixty, lined,
and weathered like an old scow.

— John Minczeski

Besides writing excellent detail for us, Minczeski also includes
similes — he makes comparisons — in this excerpt. The bags
are like anchors; the man is like a ship or a tugboat. He then
carefully describes the bags the man is carrying, his grey overcoat, rubber overshoes, the way he walks, and his face. Once
you learn how to record details and describe what you see,
smell, hear, taste, or touch, this technique can be applied to
all of your writing.

Now try writing your own description of what you see outside your window, from your porch, or what you simply
observe of a stranger while you're shopping or riding a bus.
Again, be sure to be descriptive and try to select details that
will heighten and show a mood.

Why Details Are Helpful

"Why such an emphasis on details?" you might ask. "Why
can't I just write the way I want to write?" Of course, you can.
In the long run, you probably will write the way you want to
write. And you should write as naturally and as comfortably
as you can. Writing style is like personality, and you certainly
don't want to change it. Yet, we've listed three reasons below
how details can be helpful.

- Details improve your writing.
- Details let others in.
- Details let memories surface.

Details Improve Your Writing

If someone says, "You wouldn't believe what David did. You
should have been there; it was unbelievable," we are likely to

interrupt and reply, "Well, come on. Tell me what happened."
What did David do when the waitress spilled a ladle of gravy over
him? Did he stand up and shout, "Damn it"? Or did he blush?

It's quite normal to become impatient with someone who
generalizes when talking. "Like what? Give me an example,"
we reply. Even children have a nifty way of illustrating how
important facts and details are. "Just tell me what happened!"
they shout when two children are sharing secrets.

As in conversation, we are dissatisfied with reading general-
izations. Reading, "She is beautiful," is simply not enough. We
want to see her! Is her hair long or short, curled or straight,
ribboned or flowered, braided or crimped, blond or brunette?
Comparably, "He is handsome," tells us very little. Details will
improve these otherwise bland sentences.

Details are the workhorses of all writing. All good writing—
poetry, fiction, essays, or letters—requires description and details.
Poetry requires sensuous details; a story requires a description
of dress or place for a character to become alive; thought-
provoking essays require facts to validate or clarify abstract
premises. Most of us can appreciate letters that say something;
that is, they list specific things.

Details Let Others In

There is a second reason for showing and not telling. Remember how Jack Webb often interrupted a witness and reminded
the person to give him *just* the facts. He was not interested
in the witness's conclusions, judgments, or speculations. Webb
made those himself. All he wanted were the details to help
him solve the crime and come to his own conclusion. In the
same sense, showing and detailing your thoughts and feelings
allow readers to reach their own conclusions. If you *tell* a reader
"I was happy" rather than show happiness, you are not giving the reader enough description to make his or her own
conclusion. This makes it more difficult for the reader. For the
same reason, people in Twelve Step programs describe their

own experiences and avoid giving advice so newcomers will identify more easily.

For a writing exercise, try writing a simple but detailed description of the backyard of your childhood home. Maybe it was a friend's backyard that you remember and cherish. In either case, write a short paragraph or two. We make one rule for this exercise: no words about feelings are allowed. Instead, carefully detail and describe the yard where you played; give readers a chance to sit back and visualize the scene. For example, let them hear the train barreling down the tracks behind the house where you grew up, smell the spring lilac bushes blooming in your backyard, and see clear across the wheat field. The rusted swing-set will remind them of their own. Or maybe you lived in the city and a wrought iron fire escape ran up along the side of your apartment building.

If you detail your writing carefully, the reader will have a chance to identify, to say, "That feels like home." Details make a window the reader can look through to see your world. The reader can say, "I've been there."

Here is an example written by Elizabeth Kilde Fischer who focused solely on describing a tree in her backyard.

The tree I loved grew in the woods at the end of our street, Cypress Lane. The branches lifted up like wings into another world. Sometimes I went there alone, sometimes with friends. We still had to enter this world by climbing up the boards, one at a time, nailed into the trunk. The tree was magical. Things collected in the branches. Ponies we never owned grazed in the grass below, acts of heroism fluttered from limb to limb. There were dogs and cats brought back to life, snatches of conversation floated in and out of Spanish moss. And the unnamed things and the feelings we didn't understand slept in the hollow places. The tree was never empty. And now there is a poplar tree at the edge of Lake Hiawatha. Its branches reach up like the arms of a woman dancing. There is no way for me to climb this tree. But I am a part of her. Our thoughts meet in the water where her roots grow.

— Elizabeth Kilde Fischer

All the details she's included here, such as Cypress Lane, "wings into another world," the boards nailed to the tree trunk, ponies grazing in the grass, Spanish moss, and the tree near Lake Hiawatha, connecting her to a past fantasy, contribute to creating a typical childhood scene. We can identify, even if we grew up in cities where few such trees existed in our neighborhoods. Even though she doesn't mention what she felt, we can feel the peacefulness and excitement.

Another student, AA member Greg M., once wrote a wonderful description of his Saturday afternoons pillaging the neighborhood's junkyard.

It's Saturday morning. When I reached the dump site, I was repelled by the odor of wet ashes. I grabbed a rock and hurled it into the pond behind the piles of garbage. Ka...plosh! The rock sounded like it was going down a tube when it hit the water. My eyes quickly searched the mounds of garbage for any movement. The stories I heard about rats and how large they were suddenly came back to me....The flies were intent on searching endlessly among the discarded trash. There always seemed to be one mound of trash that was smoldering. I knew if I poked at it, it would probably start to burn again. The sizes and numbers of rusted tin can lids seemed endless. The flapping pages of an open magazine caught my attention. Under it was an old pearl-covered purse with a broken zipper. I picked it up, though it appeared empty. It had a compartment inside, hid under the creased lining. I pulled the lining open and pulled out a tattered picture of a young man in a suit. The man looked happy with his wide smile and greased down hair. I was tiring and sat

down on an overturned wash tub. Rain clouds rolled
across the sky, moist cool air. . . .

— Greg M.

The description may remind you of a Saturday morning
when you wandered around your neighborhood dump. Or it
might remind you of Saturdays you drove with your father or
mother for hot chocolate and donuts. Again, he doesn't tell
you his feelings: he shows them.

Using the previous two examples for inspiration, try writing a descriptive scene from your own childhood that involves
a favorite tree or woods. If you really want to challenge yourself,
think of a place that's ugly, but where you were very happy.
As you see, even a garbage dump can serve as a topic. Whatever
you choose to write about, be as detailed as you can so others
might identify.

Details Let Memories Surface

Besides letting others in and improving the quality of your
writing, details will also focus your memory; in some cases
they will even bring long forgotten events to the surface.

Like a camera out of focus, our memory is not often clear.
Details focus the lens, and make our memories clearer, sharper,
and more powerful. For example, when we discussed back-
yards, you may have recalled a particular Cyclone fence around
your yard. Maybe it sagged at a particular spot because you
were constantly climbing over it, crunching it. It's possible that
you haven't thought of it in the last twenty years. This is how
detail brings back memories.

You may find yourself deeply moved when you discover this
ability to recall details that pierce the fog and jar the memory.
You might be suddenly startled by the clarity of a particular
memory. Write about it. Show it.

Many students have often remarked how once they started
writing more in detail, they remembered more. Some writers
say that they have always thought in their minds they knew

every detail of a particular experience, but once they started writing, more details became available. Often when they finished writing, they discovered details they hadn't even imagined. This is the magic of writing, of detailing and describing.

This ability of details to bring memories to the surface can be seen in the example below. Poet Phebe Hanson begins writing about the family's "First Car" in her book, *Sacred Hearts*.

She starts with describing her father from an old photo album.

> Here he is in an old photo album,
> my Norwegian immigrant father,
> newly-ordained graduate of Augsburg Seminary.
> *My First car - 1926,*
> he has written under the boxy Model T,
> familiar car like a child's drawing,
> home-made looking,
> a car so simple even a child
> could drive it
> and I used to pretend,
> perched on Daddy's lap,
> while we sat in the driveway
> waiting for Mother. . . .
>
> — Phebe Hanson

She goes on to mention a variety of things, such as going to camp, singing religious songs, until she remembers a particular bitter, winter night. At this point, she has completely abandoned any further description about the car and focuses on that night when "snow [was] hissing against our windshield." The father, mother, and child are standing on the shoulder of the road, hoping for someone to stop.

> ...the three of us,
> minister father in long black coat,
> mother with fur collar surround her face,
> child in blue snowsuit and aviator helmet,
> as if we were posing for a studio portrait,
> as if the swirling snow and relentless wind
> were fake backdrops in those old photographs
> where the faces radiate a strange silvery light,
> and the eyes seem to know that death's ahead
> from tuberculosis, pneumonia, diphtheria.
> We still stand in the bright blizzard light,
> frozen images by the side of the road.
> I don't remember what happened next.
> I don't remember ever being rescued.
>   — Phebe Hanson

Here we see how details lead the writer from a description of the "first car" to an eerie memory of being stuck in a near blizzard on the side of the road. Without telling us, she shows us fear, feelings of abandonment, never remembering "being rescued." One detail leads to another until a memory is jarred loose from the writer's unconscious and surfaces as another subject or image.

Try writing a similar effort. Write in prose, if you prefer. Most of us have memories involving cars. You might begin by simply describing that car. Maybe in writing this exercise, you'll discover a "deeper" memory, image, or event.

Three Common Fears about Detailing

1. "When do I get to write about truth, justice, and beauty?"

Once a student asked, "If I have to take all this time to detail my writing, when do I get to say something important? When do I get to write about truth, justice, and beauty?"

This question reveals that some students may wonder why details, say, the smell of cinnamon or the sound of faucet water dripping in the sink, are important at all.

"Who cares," the student might exclaim, "about whether I had a picket fence in my backyard or no fence at all. I want to write about addictions, incest, justice, codependency, chronic illness, life, and death."

These topics are important, and it's the *details* that will make what you have to say about them convincing and powerful. We are recognizing that you start with the window, the backyard so that you will practice and learn the skills. Then, you can handle description of more emotional scenes and make more complicated observations. Often the very "big ideas" we want to express can be found in a scene in someone's backyard.

When we are told people are starving in the world, we may simply nod our heads in agreement. But when we are shown a starving young boy, his bones protruding, his belly distended, his eye sockets sunken, we are visually shocked. We may wince and decry the situation. Seeing a bruise on a child's face repulses and angers us far more than some mathematical data that states such and such a percentage of children are abused. Being reminded by newspapers and television that murders have increased in our city by 10 percent is not nearly as frightening as actually hearing a gunshot in the vicinity of our home. What we see and hear and smell and taste and touch moves us to great depths.

2. *"I can't remember the details."*

A second fear about details is best expressed by the individual who says, "But I don't recall the details. I can't remember them." If you're a novice at writing, it might be best to stick with subjects whose details you're familiar with. Even if you don't recall the exact details, however, you can make them up as best as possible. A particular student, an older man in his sixties, once wrote a poem about playing baseball in a field back in the 1930s. To help him detail the poem, other students asked questions such as, "Well, what did you use for bases?"

The older man answered, "I don't know. I suppose we took

handfuls of wheat from the nearby field and used them for bases." Although he wasn't sure whether he did this or not, surely there is no harm in saying he did. "But then my poem won't be true," he protested. Actually, his poem was more "true" with wheat used as bases than without it because this detail helps recreate the experience in his poem and show the reader more clearly what he wants to say. The wheat shows the rural setting and the simplicity of the game.

3. *"Whenever I try to get it down on paper, I suddenly freeze."*

A third common fear writers have is in facing a blank piece of paper. A simple white sheet of paper can be a terrifying thing for some people. Especially those who approach the paper with thoughts of grandeur. Don't make writing any more difficult than it is; don't have expectations of yourself that you can't meet. Set realistic goals for yourself: one page a day, for example.

Just relax when you write, and write as if you were talking. You are actually communicating with a deeper self that desires expression as much as you do. Your memories want to be recalled. Your hurts and joys want to be shown; those experiences you couldn't find words to describe want to be shared as much as you want to share them. Writing is a kind of dialogue with another self. It's communication with another, more distant part of your self. This self is your friend. So, be open, and write honestly. Don't assume the other self knows everything. Take time to write it out. There isn't any rush.

We've talked here about three common fears people often have when asked to detail their writing more. There are probably many more fears we could discuss. But fear does not need to stop us from doing what we want. A time comes when we need to just move ahead. So, with this in mind, let's proceed to another writing exercise.

Try to Imagine Feelings as People

Early recovery in Twelve Step programs, as well as in counseling, often focuses on helping people become more aware of their feelings. Sponsors and therapists often help people identify feelings by simply allowing them to describe situations and to name the feelings they had in those situations. This task is sometimes easier said than done.

Some people can't recall what angered or hurt them; they can't remember the particular details. Sometimes they aren't even sure what feelings they had. The following writing exercise might be helpful for those of you who want to learn to better identify and name your feelings.

First, quickly write a brief list of feelings, such as embarrassment, affection, peacefulness, rage, shame, fear, or abandonment. Then, from this list, circle one to work on. For example, let's say you circled anger.

Second, imagine anger as a person. Write a description of him or her in detail. Your first impulse might be to make the person foam at the mouth; his skin could be red, his face flushed. But, consider the fact that many people do not look this way when they're angry. There are types of people whose anger is cold and quietly seething. A person dressed in a white shirt, but whose collar is tight around his neck, might be more appropriate for this type. In fact, a ripple of skin over his shirt collar could reveal how "tight" the person is. He might be gripping something — what, a handle to a briefcase? His car keys pressed into his hand, marking his palm with tiny ridges. What's his name? What could he do to "loosen up"? Remove his tie? Unbutton his collar? Have him open a refrigerator and pour himself a glass of lemonade? What might he say? These questions will be an impetus for you to describe a specific feeling as a person. Show the person's appearance, show his or her actions, gestures.

Try this exercise with other feelings. Close your eyes, and imagine a particular feeling, say hurt, as a person. Visualize hurt as a girl sitting on the edge of her bed. What color are her eyes?

Then, try to imagine fear as a woman standing in front of a mirror. She may glance up into the mirror and look behind her as she wipes her face with a washcloth.

What does your joy look like? Your gratitude? Select one feeling and begin describing it as a person.

This exercise will prove equally valuable later when we discuss inner dialogues. If you enjoy this exercise, you might move into fiction and create characters who embody particular feelings, or even concepts. We'll talk more about this later in the book.

Below, we've included a more complicated example of what this exercise is about. This is a poem by John Minczeski. He describes pain with a metaphor; pain takes on the characteristics of a person occupying another person's body, John Minczeski's sick friend. This is a good example of how effective your writing can be when you write about feelings, even pain, metaphorically and in detail. Although this example, called "Watched Clocks," is written as a poem, you may prefer to write in prose.

> First it's a small pain,
> it takes baby steps
> and then it grows up,
> it moves in
> and makes itself at home.
> I saw him then,
> his gaunt eyes
> staring up at the clock;
> the thinner he became
> (pain was grinding him down, slowly)
> the bigger the pain
> by proportion.
> Pain looked out his eyes
> from the clock, to me,
> to the window,

to the clock.
Pain flew in and out
of the window
with the resonant
architecture
of organ notes. Pain
closed his eyes
and pain opened them
with a jerk.
He thought the demerol
would kick in
in ten minutes,
then in ten minutes and ten
more. Pain was making
the clock turn around.
I kept wetting the rag
on his forehead,
and the minute hand
did as much good
as the demerol.
Pain didn't let him
talk, except in a whisper.
He asked me to stay,
and he told
the pain to go away.
But it kept seeping
into his abdominal cavity
with the minutes.
I tried to make the room
light, but it didn't help
anything. He wasn't eating,
maybe that
saved his life. "I'll
leave the tray,"
the nurse said,
"another pill?"

And now
pain looks around
the room again,
asks me
to wipe the rag
around his face
mopping up sweat,
rasping
on thick stubble.
Now pain says
Pain! go away!
but it cannot say it
strong enough
for pain to hear.
I tell him they have to pull
the ice houses
off the lakes tomorrow.
He looks at me now.
Tomorrow. He looks
at the clock, powered
by pain minutes, pain lakes,
pain melt. The month of March
is a glacier.
The eyes of pain
settle on a wall,
a humidifier, a clock,
my face, the window
with afternoon shadows
growing down from the blue,
then back to me.
You're going to write
about this, aren't you,
it says from deep
inside his eyes. I
shake my head — I can not.
Momentarily, my friend

seems to return, to relax,
but then pain simply
reaches down,
squeezes his insides
and twists so hard
he straightens like a board.
Everything is easy now,
pain seems to say,
so easy it's almost
stopped being fun anymore.

— John Minczeski

Writing Exercises Describing Twelve Step Concepts

In this section, we will look at the use of details to describe some Twelve Step concepts. Many of the principles found in Twelve Step programs come from various religions, philosophies, psychologies, and societies throughout the world. To make its wisdom more a part of your life, it might be helpful to write about the concepts using details from your real life.

Powerlessness and Unmanageability

The first of the Twelve Steps mentions the words *powerless* and *unmanageable*. You may have a good mental grasp of these concepts, but find it difficult to describe experiences in your life that illustrate these concepts. You might write, "My life was terribly unmanageable when I was drinking. I couldn't control it. Everything was going wrong. I was sad and unhappy."

Again, these examples tell how you felt, but they do not show what happened. Ask yourself: *How can I show and describe these concepts in action?*

For a writing exercise, try writing about a specific day you were drinking or using chemicals. Record the time of the day you were most likely to drink or use. Specify a particular season by simply referring to the weather. Do you recall exactly what you drank? Were other people present in the bar? Was there an overhead fan, a jukebox? Do you recall hearing the clink of ice cubes in a glass, the sound of shoes in the hall? Were you reading a newspaper article, or doing crossword puzzles while you drank alone?

What was unmanageable? Did you stay longer than you ever intended, and as a result you were late for a movie that you wanted to attend? Did you fight, argue, or become increasingly depressed? Let these questions bring details to your mind and try describing your particular drinking or using habits by showing one typical day. This next example was written by a student, an AA member named Wayne N.

> Coming out of a five month bout with booze, I was ill, frightened, and soul sick. Not being sure of who or what I was, my life had become a weird kaleidoscope of events, nothing I was doing made any sense; my marriage was on the rocks, jobs had come and gone, and my friends and I drifted together in an alcoholic haze.
>
> I remember lying on the beach in South California. My bottles of Red Ripple were lined up next to me and the sun danced and sparkled through the ruby liquid. Seagulls drifted lazily on the gentle breezes while white topped breakers roared in from the east. My eyes were heavy and my mind clogged.
>
> The next thing I remember is awakening suddenly with a mouthful of sea water and a chill that reached to my bones. The moon had taken over and the tide was cleaning the beach of all discarded trash. I jumped up, grabbed my dripping blanket and the one remaining bottle of wine and headed for home.
>
> Home was a small furnished apartment located in downtown Long Beach, California. The buildings were so close together that a car could just make it through the streets. I shared my apartment with a Swede named Dave. We had run around North America together chasing the elusive butterfly without a net and had ended

up in Long Beach. Dave had a very extroverted personality and his idea of fun was to go to a local bar and pick up strange people. Subsequently, drunken sailors and any other lost souls often ended up at our place.

Once Dave brought a Japanese sailor home whose ship had just tied up at the docks in San Pedro. He was a little man who smiled constantly and loved to get drunk on American wine....

— Wayne N.

This is a good example of focused and detailed writing. Although the first paragraph tells more than it shows, it serves as an introduction to the scenes on the beach and later at his apartment which really convey a lot through concrete sensory details. We can see how unmanageable and unpredictable his life was.

Before you begin writing your own story, we've included one more example written by a woman named Ann on her second day of chemical dependency treatment.

I have these goals: to learn how other problems in my life are related to my drug use, to write in a journal, to talk twice a week in group. . . . Is this pain any worse than getting the hell beat out of me during 18 years of marriage? I found my escape and it turned on me. Counselor says, "well, you sure showed him, didn't you? It backfired." My husband says I am hopeless and too sick to go through treatment on an outpatient basis. He has come back from a co-dependency intensive and knows all about my disease. . . . I've never been so scared or lonely. It is January 11th. Days are getting longer by minutes. Each day the sun sets a minute later, rises a minute earlier. Small changes add up to enormous ones. In February we will be surprised by light which has been growing all along. It is impossibly cold right now. I'm breathing.

— Ann

In this journal excerpt, Ann has made clear her sense of powerlessness and unmanageability. We see how she includes quotes, the *sound* of another person talking.

Try focusing, as Ann has, on some particular event that shows your life as it used to be.

Another writing exercise that might help you to describe and make more personal the First Step principles involves simply writing a list of details.

Jot down on a piece of paper concrete details that describe a particular person in your life. You might use such words as *brunette, tall, thin, a sharp nose, long fingers, high cheek bones, a thin mouth, long legs,* et cetera. Try to avoid abstract words such as *attractive, moody, stingy, or self-centered.*

After you've done this, write alongside that list details of how that person would look better. Compare the two. What do you see? How similar or different are the two lists?

Certainly you are aware that it isn't possible to change the person's actual appearance or to fit him or her to the appearance you'd like. Here, it's easy to recognize powerlessness. You may even think it's foolish to change the person in your first list into the person you desire in the second list.

A further exercise will make this exercise clearer. Write a brief list of this person's behaviors. Alongside this list, jot down the behavior you wish the person would change. Now compare the two. Note any striking differences? Circle the ones you strongly wish to have changed. Are you now as willing to acknowledge your powerlessness as you were earlier regarding the list of physical characteristics?

Normally, most people find it difficult to accept powerlessness when it concerns another person's behavior. We think we can change that person's behavior, to get him or her to stop drinking, to show more concern to us, to be more responsible or more playful.

Hopefully, this exercise will make the problems, as well as the solutions, clearer. Often, the physical act of writing, holding a pencil, forming letters into words, will make the thoughts in our minds more solid, meaningful, and effective. You might think about this exercise in your mind, but if you write it out you may end up surprised by something you hadn't even considered.

Character Defects and Shortcomings

One of the problems of dealing with the shortcomings and character defects mentioned in Step Six and Step Seven is that they may often be unclear and undefined.

Step Six: Were entirely ready to have God remove all these defects of character.

Step Seven: Humbly asked Him to remove our shortcomings.

A person may run through an abstract list of character defects such as procrastination, self-centeredness, blaming self or others, and say, "Yes, I do those things and humbly ask God to remove them." But often, people aren't conscious of just how their behavior affects everything else. Subsequently, the character defects haven't really been identified.

First, list in general terms a few of your character defects. Second, select one and begin *detailing* or describing yourself when that character defect is in action. Use strong nouns and active verbs involving your five senses that *show* and describe you. Select a specific location where this takes place. For example, if you are dealing with procrastination, you might write something like this.

The letter remains unopened on the dining room bureau. Every morning, I pass it on the way to the kitchen to make myself a cup of coffee. I sit at the breakfast table thinking about the letter. I say to myself, "right after breakfast, I'm going to open the letter and write a reply." The letter is from my ex-wife and something I can't name keeps me from opening it. Yet, after I finish my coffee, eat my bowl of cereal, and rinse out the dishes, I walk back through the living room, pass the bureau with the letter lying on it, and shuffle back up-stairs in my slippers. This goes on day after day.

What do we see in this example? Verbs that describe action such as making coffee, eating cereal, shuffling in slippers, sitting at a table. We know the letter is from the writer's ex-wife and lies on the dining room bureau. We don't know why he just doesn't open the letter and write a reply, only that he doesn't. The writer is simply describing what he does when he procrastinates. When you write your description of a particular character defect, don't think that you must resolve the situation.

When writing, people often feel compelled to write a solution, an appropriate end. You don't have to. Sometimes a detailed description will steer you into the direction of acceptance. Then, a solution might be possible. Once you "see" how you procrastinate or act out shortcomings, they become more real and, at the same time, less haunting because, through acceptance, the shortcomings exert less control over your life.

Higher Power

Many of the Twelve Steps refer to a Higher Power. Step Twelve speaks of a spiritual awakening.

> Having had a spiritual awakening as the result of these steps, we tried to carry this message to alcoholics, and to practice these principles in all our affairs.

The following writing exercise is aimed at helping you describe and deepen your understanding of a Higher Power.

One day, while flying from Chicago, a four-year-old child, flying in a plane for the first time, looked out the window to see the blue sky, the white, fluffy clouds and said, "That's where we go when we die. Blackie, my puppy, is in those clouds playing." She paused for a moment as she continued to stare out the window and turned back to her father sitting beside her. "How come I can't see God out there?" she asked.

This little child is questioning her own understanding of God. If heaven is "up there" in the clouds, then God must be there and, if so, why can't she see God? What would He or She look like?

Using this anecdote to help you explore your understanding of a Higher Power, try describing and detailing your understanding of a Higher Power or God using words from the senses. Words such as *All-present, All-knowing, omnipotent* found in old Baltimore catechisms are not words that you can observe, taste, smell, touch, or hear. Here's a brief example using details that involve the senses.

> My Higher Power fills the ocean, and swirls the colorful leaves into spiraling circles. God is the taste of a plum. Or an open eye weeping in the night sky surrounded by the glittering glass of broken stars and hopes. As well as the shadows lying under an oak tree, the rain soaking the ground under a child's bare feet, the pulse in my wrist...

This exercise may help you deepen and clarify your understanding of a Higher Power. The images you create may help you to see how present and available your Higher Power is to you. You might be surprised by the images and details you write.

After you've done this exercise, choose one particular detail and develop it. Using the previous example, the writer might select "the pulse in my wrist." The writer could develop this image by including other things that have rhythms, such as the heart, a drum, a clock, crickets, rain pattering, even a neon light flickering.

Another exercise centers around people's general uneasiness in selecting a pronoun for God. Here's an example where one writer explored this problem.

> My God follows me as I drive down Wichita Street. It used to matter what I called God and that I punctuate correctly, using capital letters whenever I used

pronouns referring to God. I didn't like telling people that I would turn to the backseat and talk to *Him*. My God is not a He, nor is my God a She, or an It. My God doesn't have breasts, yet my God nourishes and lets me suckle when I am trapped like a child in a traffic jam. God doesn't smell like a working man yet my God loves the odor of sweat and looking out across manure fields as far and wide as the horizon. God is not a mother on earth, yet God is the corn, wheat, and soybeans. God is not a father, yet the seeds scattered by the combines down plowed rows are Gods. . . .

Try describing your Higher Power using both the pronoun *He* and *She*. Describe both the male aspects and female aspects of your Higher Power.

Your own description will be lasting, and you'll be able to summon it into your mind whenever you need to feel more in touch with your Higher Power.

CHAPTER 4

Collecting the Ingredients: Making Lists

What a wealth of materials we have to work with! Staples like milks and stocks, oils, beans, sprouts, honeys, gelatins, leavens, cheese and eggs, nuts, seeds, herbs, and exotics like chocolates and spices.

— Irma S. Rombauer
and Marion Rombauer Becker
The Joy of Cooking

Everyone makes lists. List making is such a common human activity that perhaps it is not often recognized as writing. A person making a list may say, "Oh, this is just my way of getting organized." It is a way of getting organized, but it can also be a part of writing for recovery. Listing is useful. It's also a skill you probably already have.

Let's think about the nature of lists. What do they do for you? When you're getting ready to go grocery shopping, you may walk through the kitchen and see what's there. You take stock of what's there and take notes. You jot down ideas for shopping. You let your imagination roam around and think about what would be good to eat. You think about staples you need to keep a supply of. You may sit down with a cookbook, leaf through, and look for a new, appealing recipe.

You make a list in no particular order. You may add comments like, "snacks for the picnic," or "whatever fruit looks ripest." You don't worry about interspersing personal comments between the milk and eggs and lettuce. You're inconsistent because the list is private. A list is easy to add on to. It goes on and on, unlike a story that has a beginning, middle, and end. A list is timeless, eternal, endless, yet bound to a certain moment in time.

Looked at from another point of view, we can say that a shopping list is a compact, compressed nugget of information about our present life. It is the skimpy snatch of a life from which you may see a bigger picture.

Now think about what a list can give you. It's a summary of what you need, want, or have, or see at a particular moment in time. It's a survey, an overview, a summary of the crucial facts of the state of one aspect of your life. It's a kind of blueprint that can be a guide to the future.

A list is always an archaeological find. Much of our information about how people lived in other times has come from mundane pieces of writing, such as diaries that consisted of shopping lists, records of trips to town, reports on the harvest, et cetera. Ancient stone tablets may show lists of the monarch's holdings in the exchange of the time, such as wine or gold.

You might play archaeologist with a short list. Read the following list and draw conclusions about the person, family life, consciousness, politics, physical health, clothes, feelings. Be playful and outrageous when you think of who wrote this list. . .what season is it?

> whole wheat fig newtons
> doz eggs, no styrofoam cartons, try to remember
> cantelopes go by food coop if the melons are green
> pinto beans tell Heather if she doesn't eat the beans
>   we'll go back to hamburgers

frozen pizza
marshmallows, graham crackers, Hershey bars
trail mix — how many people coming along?

Before you read any further, take a minute to talk about this list with a friend or write out a description of the author of the list.

Lists as Symbolic Writing

In this grocery list and your reflections on it, you can see how a list is a slice of life that represents a larger life. In this way, a list is a symbol of a world greater than itself.

Some people carry lists as a symbol, as a talisman. Some people in Twelve Step programs say that they like to carry their group's telephone list with them at all times. The list conjures up the picture of the group. Looking at the telephone list with its ordinary names and numbers suggests the other people who are alive, struggling. The list suggests thoughts and inspiration that give comfort.

You need to remember all this power that a list can have and not diminish it as a source of writing. You don't want to minimize your writing ability by saying, "All I do is make lists." Making lists can be a rich source for your writing and a source of clarity and growth.

- You can make a list of feelings to discover how you're feeling.
- You can make a list of pleasures as a way to create more pleasure in your life.
- If you're stuck in a conflict or feeling trapped, you can make a list of choices.
- If you want to face and accept your present situation, you can make a list of all your losses, to help you let acceptance into your consciousness.
- You can make a list that reveals a world view that is both unified and allows for ambivalences.

One of our favorite examples is an anonymous list that was passed out at a Twelve Step meeting. We like it for its combination of seriousness and humor.

SOME SIGNS AND SYMPTOMS OF INNER PEACE

Tendency to think and act spontaneously rather than from fears based on past experience.

An unmistakable ability to enjoy each moment.

Loss of interest in judging other people.

Loss of interest in judging self.

Loss of interest in interpreting the actions of others.

Loss of ability to worry. (This is a very serious symptom.)

Frequent, overwhelming episodes of appreciation.

Contented feelings of connectedness with others and nature.

Frequent attacks of smiling through the eyes from the heart.

Increasing tendency to let things happen rather than make them happen.

Increased susceptibility to love extended by others as well as the uncontrollable urge to extend it.

Warning: If you have all of even most of the above symptoms, please be advised that your condition of PEACE may be so far advanced as not to be curable.

— Anonymous

List Making as a Warm-Up for Writing

Writers often use list making as a warm-up activity. Lists are similar in effect to stream-of-consciousness writing in that we can go on and on without worrying about where we're going. Many writers we know make lists of

- Favorite words
- What I want to write about
- Words I don't understand
- Words I hate, like "to access"
- Images that are still mysterious to me
- Lines that come out of nowhere
- Books I've read
- Details from observing a scene
- Overheard conversations
- Words I want to get better at, like words I can use to describe smells

These are working lists for writers. There are many more kinds of lists that could be useful to you as a writer. Some writers keep a special place in their journal or notebook for their current working lists. We should say, too, that preference for listing seems to be a function of personality. Not everybody likes to make lists. Some writers never make lists. Others live with them on a daily basis. Try making a list now; use one of the ideas above to get started.

The listing that you do for writing warm-ups may later be the source for a story, a poem, an essay. A list may yield many kinds of writing, just as a grocery sack of ingredients could turn into a vegetable soup, a spinach soufflé, or a cold salad.

Five Kinds of Lists

What we want to look at in this chapter are some of the ways that list making can be used in the recovery process. We have drawn on the work of many people in our thinking about this process. We've divided listing as a process into five categories.

- Emergency Lists
- Lists for Self-Discovery
- Lists for Understanding New Concepts
- Lists that Work Over Time
- Collections

Then we will discuss how listing can be of use when working the Steps.

Emergency Lists

For those of us who have a chronic problem — with negative feelings, mental health, suicidal thoughts, or addictions — listing can be helpful. For example, if we have a problem isolating ourselves from other people, we could make two lists. The first one could include how to recognize our own isolation, and the second one could include ways to break the isolation. Having lists is helpful in this way: when we are in a downward spiral, we forget what we know. We panic, go blank, split, numb out. If we have a list — in a familiar place, like the first page of a journal, or taped on the wall by the phone — we are more likely to catch ourselves before we fall all the way down the tunnel into the pit. People have their own danger signs; they are different for each person. A person with suicidal thoughts might have on the list things to watch for, such as an inability to get out of bed, dread, letting one wrong thing ruin everything else. A person in a Twelve Step program may rely on *H.A.L.T.* as a warning list — Hungry, Angry, Lonely, or Tired.

The second list, the list for what to do, will be very individual. It might start with a phone number of a friend who knows what the chronic problem is. The list can continue with activities that nurture, that help you get grounded again, that give you hope. There is a wonderful list called "Things to Do When I'm Desperate" in the book *The Courage to Heal: A Guide for Women Survivors of Child Sexual Abuse,* by Ellen Bass and Laura Davis. The first thing to do on this list is *Breathe.*

Take some time now and make a list for yourself.

Lists for Self-Discovery

Of course, we could say that all listing — and all writing — is a process of self-discovery.

What we are talking about in this section is writing with the intention of becoming more clear about who we are — the discovery of our truer selves.

Try this exercise as a warm-up right now. Take five minutes and list all the feelings you have today. For example, you may list single words or you may explain exactly what you mean by the word *jealous:* "so jealous I could burn my food stamps." You may be inconsistent! You may be contradictory. The list will be unified because of the time and place and who you are today.

At the end of your five minutes writing time, you will be able to survey the richness of your emotional life.

Here are some ways you could use the list you just made to write more.

- Circle the strongest feeling and list details that further describe that feeling.
- Refer to writing about feelings in the chapters on description (Chapter Three) and altered point of view (Chapter Six).
- Think of synonyms for all the feelings you've listed; that might give you another slant to them.
- If a forgotten memory emerged while you were writing, make a few notes about this memory at the bottom of the page.
- Make a new list of all the times you've experienced this strongest feeling.

Writing about feelings in a list is a way to connect with your unconscious. It's a telescope that lets you get in touch with what's going on at any given moment. One great thing about lists is that you don't need elaborate equipment. If you don't have your journal with you, you can write lists on anything: napkins, backs of envelopes, or check deposit slips. Listing as a spot check can include questions like: What are my priorities today? What do I need to take care of? What can I do this evening to be at peace? If you are feeling confused, anxious, or blocked, you can write quickie lists to get clear.

Pleasure Lists

Listing for self-discovery also includes a slower way of working. We might start a pleasure list for something we don't know the answer to. For example, What are my favorite words? What do I like to do for fun? How many ways do I know how to relax? What are my favorite foods? What are some healthy ways to express my sensuality? Asking questions we don't know the answer to is a way to get acquainted with our sources of well-being.

Sometimes these lists fall into the form of a poem before we are even aware that this is happening. Words scattered on a page can suddenly coalesce into a shape in the same way that metal filings suddenly align themselves into a pattern when touched by a magnet.

We'll look at two lists that suddenly emerged as poems. The first is from a list of favorite words.

LOVE OF WORDS

interweave
moon
brindled
woven
gentle
abandon
canticle
shimmer

trickle
  inlet
pianissimo
  opaque
coddle
  lovely
caprice
  spiral
arpeggio
  grey
sphere
  bough
ivory
  hallowed
keel
  whirling
translucent
  cleave
soothe
  halo
woodwind
  dwindle
sinuous
  dazzling
supple
  furrow
whisper
  below
braiding
  Iroquois
muffled
  yellow

— Elizabeth Kilde Fischer

What we see in the selection from this poem is a mysterious weaving of words with *w's* and *n's* and *d's,* as well as the repetition of certain vowel sounds. The writer is responding to sounds in the world that she loves. What does the poem mean? We would hesitate to put a meaning on it. But we can know something about the self that is discovered through these sounds and words. A musical person. A person with a sensitive response to the world.

The second list plays with two lists. One list is for words that are synonyms for straight, and the other is for words that are not straight. What meanings do you associate with the word *straight*? It has a variety of meanings: sober (not high), middle class, conformist, heterosexual, and a person with a rigid personality. *Not straight* is the opposite of all these meanings. This next writer explores her own connotations, without telling us exactly which meanings she's talking about. We have to decide that for ourselves.

straight/not straight

1. the ruler's metal edge
   beside the pencil line, the face
   betraying no emotion, deadpan,
   actor serving as a foil
   for the comedian,
   the military posture,
   puritanical, the corset
   cinched up tight,
   a jacket binding arms
   against the body
   as a means of restraint.

2. wriggling of a garden
   snake, the natural curl
   of pea vines, lines
   of female form,
   a kite tail wagging,

> lazy sway of one leaf falling,
> goldfinch flight,
> the whorls within a fingerprint,
> crooked necks of yellow squash,
> a change in one's direction,
> course of sailboats in the wind.
>
> — Grace Caroline Bridges

Now we'd like you to make a list. Use one of the two ideas we just discussed. Either write out a list of words you love, or write a list of words you associate with *straight/not straight*. If you like playing around with lists like these, as we do, read the chapter on poetry (Chapter Nine), where we discuss lists and chants in more detail.

Lists for Understanding New Concepts

When we're learning new concepts, experiencing a paradigm shift, trying out new behaviors, "acting as if," writing can help us find clarity of thought. When we write, we free-associate, think, try new words. We can pick a concept we don't yet understand and ask, *"What does this word suggest? What did it used to mean to me? What does it mean now?"*

One way to get at our understanding of words is to write a list of what a word suggests to us. Sometimes we can use the dictionary as a starting point. We can list all the synonyms and think about which ones really work for us. For people in recovery, some words typically change in their meaning. Some of these words are: fun, love, dependency, sexuality, self, friends, spirituality, work, a good time.

Take a few minutes now, put the book down, and select one of the above words. Make a list of meanings for it. Or, you could make two lists: one list of what you used to think the word meant, and a second list of what it means to you now.

This process can be a helpful activity for new words you encounter on the path of spiritual growth. Here is the work of one woman in her struggle with her comprehension of the word *codependency.* Her list became an abstract poem as she worked on it.

REVELATIONS

Codependence
means dependence
on a cooperative coalition
between two parties
codependent on one another
one strong, the other weak
each finding their coexistence better than taking
the risks of aloneness

This dependency on me
is a connection
with being needed, indispensable
I will never be
left behind
codependence looks generous
I look strong and responsible
but underneath I am scared
and have learned to fight my infantile fear by
encouraging others to need me

Generous?
No, selfish and egocentric
all for the sake of peace for the moment peace for me
— Emily White

We mentioned that you might start your list using the dictionary and thinking about the many meanings of a word. Sometimes people take a list and write about it. For example, here is a short article that we can see probably started with a list from the dictionary.

COMPASSION RUN AMUCK

"Codependency" can be a confusing term. I have found it helpful to think of it as "compassion run amuck."

"Amuck" comes from the Malaysian word, "amoq," which means "engaging furiously in battle," so the expression "to run amuck" means "to rush about in a frenzy to kill, or to commit violent acts."

To have compassion, on the other hand, is to "suffer with another; to have sorrow for the distress or misfortunes of another, with a desire to help."

It has been my experience that when I am behaving codependently, my compassion is running amuck. I know I am being codependent when I find myself engaging furiously in the suffering of another, and rushing about in frenzied sorrow for the distress or misfortunes of that person, with a sincere desire to help. Or to commit violent acts.

— Anne Jefferies

This same process can be helpful in our relationships with other people. In his book *Stage II Relationships: Love Beyond Addiction*, Earnie Larson talks about one way he and his wife work together to bring about more empathy in their relationship. They've made a list they call "Significant Words," and every week they pick one to focus on. Each person writes about it, meditates on it, and then they get together and share their views. Some of the words on their list are: *vacation, competition, money, sex.*

Make a list now of your "Significant Words." This can be a list from which you can select a word a week to concentrate on, either alone or with a partner.

We'll explain one more way of working with lists as a way of understanding concepts. This is a process for looking at and changing the messages you received in your family of origin.

When we work with kids in schools, we call it *The Bossy Poem*. First, make a list of all the messages you received in your childhood about how to be. Messages such as: *Be neat, Be smart, Be nice, Be tough.* As you write, you can also think of the *Don't be's* that always accompany the *be's*, such as *Don't be a smart-aleck, Don't be the center of attention, Don't be a cry baby.* Another way to get at this material is to ask yourself what it was that your parents most feared you'd become. A hippie? A draft dodger? A Republican? A bum? A childless career woman? All of these answers have surfaced in our classes.

You might also ask yourself, *What messages did I receive about gender roles? Don't be a sissy* (said to boys), *Don't be too smart* (said to girls), are messages about gender.

After you've made a long list of messages, circle the message that seems to have exerted the most powerful hold on your life, a message that you want to change. Many of the childhood messages are ones we want to keep. This exercise is concerned with changing the ones we don't want.

Now it's time to write *The Bossy Poem*. Pretend you are the voice of The Boss, the parent, the culture at large, ordering a small child around. Make another list of all the actions that go along with being and not being this way. When you have a list that's at least a page long, play with the order of the words to get at a rhythm. The list should skate along, with an insistent beat, leaving no time for back talk. Here is an example which was written by Roseann Lloyd.

EXORCISM OF NICE

Mum's the word
Taciturn
Talk polite
Appropriate
Real nice
Talk polite
Short and Sweet
Keep it down

Quiet down
Keep the lid on
Hold it down
Shut down
Shut up
Chin up
Bottle up
Drink up
Up-tight
Tied up in knots
Tight-lipped
Hold tight
Tongue-tied
Hold your tongue
Hold still
Hold it back
Hold it in
Hold your cards close to your chest
Close-mouthed
Muzzled
Gagged
Garbled
Jammed up
All wrapped up
Tied up
Shut up
Zonked out
Tucked in
Caved in
Shut in
Locked in
Incoherent
Inarticulate
In a shell
Shell-shocked
Thunder-struck

Dumb-struck
Stupefied
Shut-down
Stunned

Oh, Wicked Mother of the Kingdom of Silence
I have obeyed you
long enough.

— Roseann Lloyd

Lists that Work Over Time

The lists we've talked about so far in this chapter can be completed in a few minutes or a few hours. They're a quick way to zero in on a feeling, a concept. Of course, you could spend more time on them, but the point is you don't have to in order to accomplish a lot. You can get a lot out of them in a short time.

The lists we'll look at in this section are lists that we set up with the intention of using over a long period of time. Lists that we live with. Lists that are part of a continuing process of spiritual work. They work over time because they are part of a daily spiritual practice.

What kind of work needs time? The work that is slow to unfold. The work we instinctively know we can't do in a day or a month. For example, one student was having trouble accepting all the losses that had happened in her life. She made a list of losses to let herself see all the losses and to accept them as reality. Her process reminds us of a scene in a recent television show, *St. Elsewhere,* where one of the main characters, a nurse who has been divorced several times, sees her daughter being brought in after a suicide attempt. She blurts out, "This is not the life I wanted." How many of us have thought the same thing? The thought can rise to the surface even after years of work in therapy and recovery programs, and it has many names — resistance, lack of acceptance, lack of trust, denial. Keeping a list of losses is a way to work through our lack of acceptance. Maybe it would help acceptance to call this list the *Acceptance List* rather than the *Loss List*.

Another list, the opposite of loss, is a list of things we have gratitude for. After any loss, discovering and regaining the feeling of gratitude is a slow process. A list that we can add on to slowly may help us let in gentle, thankful feelings. In fact, any concept or feeling that you would like to have but feel resistant to can become a list that works over time. This list can focus on the following ideas.

- A list imagining global peace
- A list of wonderful experiences you want to have when you retire
- A list of joys you want to experience today
- A list of good things you notice in your world

The writer Larry Block suggests in his book *Write for Your Life* that people who want to write should make a list of one hundred things they want. His idea is that we need to visualize ourselves as deserving of many gifts in order to feel that we deserve the *time* we will need to become writers. This is a tough assignment. As authors of this book, both of us are doing all the exercises we recommend to others, and we admit that this one is one of the toughest. As people who came of age in the anti-materialistic 1960s, we have still not finished our list of one hundred things. But we will! This is definitely a list that works over time.

Another list that works over time is the old-fashioned prayer list. This is a list of people we want to remember to send good energy to, during quiet moments of meditation. As we discuss in the chapter on affirmations and prayers (Chapter Five), not everyone is comfortable with the word *prayer*; it seems that the word for prayer in the 1980s is *visualization*. If this is your preference, you could keep a list of people to visualize and send energy to. The list may change often, as long as it continues to be a list that is in use.

Before you leave this section, choose one of our suggestions as an assignment to take with you: *Acceptance List, Gratitude List, Joy List, One Hundred Things I Want List, Prayer-Visualization List*. Make a decision to work on the list by writing in at least three items today.

Collections: Picking Up Rocks on the Beach

We've all probably collected rocks on the beach — shells, pretty things we find outside that have no apparent use. It seems to be human nature to collect, to want to add on, add on. We can do it with words too. It is easier to collect words than to collect antique automobiles, although our book-filled basements, shelves, and desks may attest to the obsessive nature of word collecting also.

When we love words and writing, we find that we can collect them in special ways. For example, you may start collecting quotes that you love. You may write them down in your journal. Then you have trouble finding them, mixed in with all your ramblings, grocery lists, notes to yourself, memories, inventories, et cetera. So you go out and buy a special blank book, and keep this book only for your quotes. You no longer have a list of favorite quotes; you have a collection.

One therapist asked his client to go out and buy a scrapbook and label it, "My 'Take Credit' Book." The client was instructed to write a paragraph on a page every time something good happened — every time someone expressed appreciation for his spirit, or thanked him for something kind he did. As you might imagine, this client was having trouble with self-esteem. He was having trouble accepting and receiving love. Maybe we could all benefit from this activity, even if we have not been identified as having low self-esteem. Why not get out a notebook and start your own 'Take Credit' book today?

There are many other ways to use lists, to collect them, to channel this potentially obsessive love into a natural high. *The New Diary*, by Tristine Rainer, offers other ideas for listing.

Collect Your Favorite Things in a Travel Sack

If you were going on an imaginary journey, what would you take with you? You may bring words, quotes, objects, landscapes, sounds, colors, books. The writer, Susan Campbell, got the idea for this next poem from a class taught by Carolyn Forche, who in turn got the idea from a poem by the Greek writer, Odysseas Elytis, who has been awarded the Nobel Prize for his unusual, innovative poems. Here is an excerpt from Susan Campbell's poem.

TRAVEL SACK

Antonio Marchado
   Walker there is no path.
   You make the path while you walk.

Pablo Neruda
   "Ode to My Socks"

Georgia O'Keeffe
   The Grey Hills (1942)
      I have to get my clothes in my drawers in
      order before I can paint. Don't even think
      you won't succeed.

Bach
   Violin Concerto in D

Fausch
   Pacalbel Canon in D

Elizabeth Bishop
   There is always the possibility of finding
   home.

Aldo Leopold
   A Sand County Almanac

Barry Lopez
Artic Dreams
River Notes

Wendell Berry
I come into the presence of still water and I
feel above me the day-blind stars

Kawishiwi River
Sound of heron's wings
Loon cries at dark

Anne Cameron
Daughters of Copper Woman

— Susan Campbell

What would your "travel sack" contain? Your list may include all the richness of the world. All you have to do is start, start with one book, one bird, one word you love. Start to fill your travel sack now.

Lists and the Twelve Steps

The Twelve Steps encourage people to use lists. The word *list* is mentioned directly in Step Eight. The word *inventory* is used in Step Four and Step Ten. Many Twelve Step members have used listing in their work with Step One. Why is listing useful when working the Steps?

To answer that question, we return to the idea of the shopping list. Making a list involves a survey of what is available, what is in stock. Only when we see what we have on the kitchen shelves can we decide what it is we need to buy. Making a list shows objectively what is and what isn't in stock.

Listing is a way to see clearly, to see the whole picture, to break through denial, to cut through endless anecdotes, rambling, and detours. A list is like a map; it's on one piece of paper. It sums up.

In this section, we'll look at Step One, Step Four, Step Eight, and Step Ten. You can use this section as a resource when you are working on a particular Step.

Step One: "We admitted we were powerless over alcohol — that our lives had become unmanageable."

Making a list for Step One can be done from several different points of view: you can focus on powerlessness, or on loss of control, on unmanageability, on dependency. Simply put the words at the top of a piece of paper and start listing. If you want to focus on loss of control, start listing, for example, nights you started out intending to have two beers and ended up at midnight with seven Black Russians, or the times you were late getting to the day-care center because you stopped for a drink and it turned into four drinks. Don't worry about chronology. List events in any order, any year. In the process, everything else about your life falls by the wayside; that is, you don't put down anything about feelings, excuses, extenuating circumstances. The list contains only events that occurred. The list also leaves out your present feelings about the events. Shame, embarrassment, loneliness, and regret are not a part of this list, although they may be part of another list at some other time. This list will speak for itself. The point here to discover for yourself the extent of your loss of control; to cut through your denial and to look honestly at your behavior.

As you write, you may experience anxiety. The point is to keep writing regardless of feelings. The point is to get all this on paper so that it can be seen clearly. This is self-discovery at its most painful. But you will work through the pain and the shame.

Remember the shopping list? When you survey your kitchen, you take the position of an observer who is not judgmental. You note that you are out of dried beans and ketchup. You don't start making judgments about who ate all the ketchup. (If you do, you may not make it to the grocery store today.) You also refrain from making judgments about whether pinto beans are better than kidney beans — the point is you're out of beans.

In the same way, you can write about your powerlessness over addiction without making judgments. List what has happened. This is not easy to do, but the form of the list helps because it doesn't leave much room for sentences.

Other ways to focus on Step One include listing the money you spent on your addiction, time you spent away from family and friends, problems at work, and dangerous and life-threatening situations you've been involved with. It is important to state that every addiction eventually involves life-threatening behaviors. Each of these lists casts another light on powerlessness and unmanageability.

Which list "should" you pick to write about? Whenever we are writing, we follow unconscious leads: we write about whatever leaps off the page at us. If you want to do a Step One list, let yourself follow the one word on this page that has jumped out at you. Maybe the word is *dangerous*, maybe the word is *family*. Follow that word.

However you choose to work with Step One, listing can bring you closer to knowing yourself. Step One is the path to knowing yourself as you really are.

Step Four: "Made a searching and fearless moral inventory of ourselves."

Step Four is the first time in the Twelve Steps that a list is referred to. In practice, the word *inventory* means writing a list, even though the Step doesn't say this directly. An inventory is like a grocery list. It is a survey of your present spiritual life: behaviors and feelings that are barriers to love. It is a survey of behaviors that cause harm to ourselves and others. If this Step is causing fear, as it often does, it is useful, again, to go back and think of the inventory of the kitchen. Taking an inventory means looking to see what you have.

Remember you do not judge who ate the ketchup; instead you write down *out of ketchup*.

Many books on the Twelve Steps talk in great detail about how to do a Fourth Step so we won't go on too long here. The book, *The Twelve Steps for Everyone (Who Really Wants Them)* summarizes several approaches to the Fourth Step from various Twelve Step programs. The book *Alcoholics Anonymous*, usually referred to as The Big Book, suggests listing troublesome feelings, especially fears and resentments, as well as behaviors. Starting on page sixty-four of The Big Book, a process is outlined that is based on list making.

We want to emphasize that listing is a liberating experience. It works with the Fourth Step the same way it works with the First Step. No matter how long a list is, it's still a list; what you do is add on, add on, add on. You can make a list that surveys your life completely without ever venturing into the world of essays, letters, stories, or poems.

The Fourth Step, like the grocery list, is a survey of your present spiritual health. It is free of judgment. It lets you become free to move on.

Step Eight: "Made a list of all persons we had harmed and became willing to make amends to them all."

Step Eight is a list. It is a list that works over time. Many people interpret this Step to mean that the list should be made during the Fourth Step. Sometimes people don't do that and wait to make a list until they have worked through the first seven Steps. However you interpret the Steps, it's important to note that the only thing required in Step Eight is to have a list and become willing. No other action is required.

What does it mean in this day and age to make a list? Mainly it means to make it, to keep track of it, and to remember where it is. Many people get stuck here simply because the list disappears. It seems that figuring out how not to "lose" the list may be one way to increase willingness. Keeping track of the list validates willingness.

Many people in the program have a notebook for lists like a Step Eight list and a prayer list. But as is often the case, the need to destroy a list is often as strong as the need to keep a list. Many people feel the need to destroy, burn, or otherwise get rid of their Fourth Step list as a ritual that symbolizes forgiveness after they've done their Fifth Step. Because of this need, it is important to sort out what can be burned and what is important to keep.

Willingness comes, too, from paying attention to process.

Making Lists Can Offer Healing in Step Ten: "Continued to take personal inventory and when we were wrong promptly admitted it."

The more often you do Step Ten, the less often life will get so complicated that you need to do a Fourth Step inventory. In practice, most people in the program interpret the word *continued* to mean *on a daily basis*. But it doesn't say *daily*. It says *continued*, meaning *as a part of living*. When you do this is probably a matter of individual temperament, lifestyle, morning grumpiness, and work schedule.

Many publishing companies and Twelve Step programs put out cards with a list of a daily moral inventory. These may be useful, but often people write their own lists. A personal list often focuses on issues the person is presently working on.

Basically, Step Ten asks, "How am I doing?" One person in the program looks at his life in terms of overall categories: emotional, spiritual, social, physical, and intellectual. He evaluates his progress each evening. Another person works with a series of questions, which she asks herself each morning, as a guide for the day.

• What do I need to do for my recovery today?
• What am I feeling today?
• Is there any reality I need to check out concerning my feelings?
• Is there any action I need to take care of today?

- What are my priorities today?
- Just for today, what comes first?
- Have I set aside time I need for relaxation, fun, and meditation?
- What is my own thought for the day, to guide me?

Her guiding thought is one from the Gospel of Thomas as quoted in *The Gnostic Gospels,* by Elaine Pagels: *Do not lie and do not do what you hate.*

Before you read any further, you might take a few minutes to write a list of your questions. What questions could help you be centered each morning? What thought is closest to your heart and mind?

To conclude the work in this chapter, you might make a list for yourself of two thoughts that give you comfort and inspiration. These may be your own thoughts or quotes from someone else. Put this list somewhere where you will find it when you wake up tomorrow.

CHAPTER 5

Diamonds in the Rough: Writing Affirmations, Meditations, and Prayers

You your best thing, Sethe. You are.
— Toni Morrison

If the only prayer you say in your life is "thank you," that would suffice.
— Meister Eckhart

We are all diamonds in the rough. Our work with affirmations, meditations, and prayers is a way to mine deeper and release our true selves. This writing work is also a tool for becoming the people we want to become.

The image of the diamond is a transforming image. Diamonds, and all gems, do not shine and reflect light when they are in their natural state. It is only after they are cut that their facets emerge in their symmetrical design; only after they are faceted and polished that they have the power to reflect light and shine. We could even say that a stone has to be broken before it can shine. We use the word *broken* in this context to connect the stone and the human. Many of us use the word *broken* to describe the damage that has been done to us and the damage that we have done. But *brokenness* as a condition of living has its gifts. In the process of healing, we may find greater depths of compassion and kindness than we had previously.

So we use the image, the picture, of a cut, faceted stone as an image to begin this work. Diamonds, of course, have other associations that may be negative for you. If you have these negative images, we suggest finding another stone that is positive for you, such as a ruby, a tiger eye, a star opal.

Affirmations Bring out Positive Energy

Many people, in a variety of fields, have worked with affirmations in the last twenty years. Books have proliferated on this subject. This work connects with work being done on guided imagery, relaxation, and other techniques for changing the unconscious beliefs we want to try to change. Books that may be useful include *Creative Visualization* by Shakti Gawain, and *Loving Relationships* and *The Only Diet There Is*, both by Sondra Ray.

Working with affirmations always involves writing. It may also involve talking, thinking, musing, praying, but it always includes writing as a crucial step in the process. For it is in the process of writing down affirmations and then finding the one that resonates most strongly, that we discover our deepest needs and desires. As an example of this, we'll talk about Mark G., who is changing his view of himself and his attitudes about money. He has decided to work with the affirmation, *I am now experiencing abundance.* As he writes the affirmation, his mind is free to wander and think of objections. This wandering is part of the process. He hears a voice that says, *Then how come you bounced three checks last month?* Now bouncing three checks may or may not have anything to do with abundance, but it's linked in his mind. In this way, Mark discovers how his mind is working. Sondra Ray says of this process, "Love brings forth that which is unlike itself." When we write affirmations, we are practicing self-love, and our negativity will have to emerge. Mark learns during his writing time that he needs to deal with his checkbook in a more organized way before he can feel and acknowledge the abundance in his life.

Sondra Ray quotes the Bible when she says that we need to write out affirmations not seventy times, but seven times seventy. Jesus said that is how many times we should forgive someone. Maybe we think this idea sounds punitive. But perhaps the words are not a prescription, but a *description* of how hard it is for humans to change deeply held beliefs. Anyone who has tried to forgive someone can attest to the difficulty of forgiveness. And when we write out our affirmations, we see that seven times seventy is not too little.

Affirmations show us how writing as a process works. As we write, our mind goes all over the place. We may think of the saying, *Trust the Process.*

An example of the process we can trust is shown in the story of Jennifer K., a compulsive overeater. She grew up in a perfectionistic family in which women were expected to be neat, well-groomed, and slender to the point of anorexia. Her father had high expectations for his wife and daughters. Jennifer grew up feeling that she never looked good enough and never had her father's approval.

As part of her Twelve Step program, she worked on forgiveness. Forgiveness for herself, for internalizing her father's misogyny. Forgiveness for her father.

At first, she had to deal with her own willingness to forgive. When she was ready, she started writing the affirmation *I forgive my father completely.* Writing this seven times seventy, she realized that she was actually writing *I forgive the fathers completely.* Plural. All the fathers. It was only at this point in her work that she got in touch with her tremendous anger at a culture that tells us that a "woman" is a creature with the anorexic body of a ten-year-old. Jennifer's writing brought her closer to healing, because it brought her clarity about her full, true, cleansing anger.

"Do you know," she says, "it takes three people to put one skinny model into the blue jeans that are in magazine ads?

That's how tight the jeans are." She reminds us of a wonderful quote from Isadora Duncan.

> . . . I am glad that I was young in a day when people were not so self-conscious as they are now. In those days, THIN was not equivalent to spirituality.
> — Isadora Duncan

Here are step-by-step instructions for writing and using affirmations. These particular instructions, which differ only slightly from others, come from a Hazelden pamphlet by Brenda Schaeffer, *Love Addiction: Help Yourself Out.* These directions are the clearest we have found. Affirmations are especially important when you hear your mind saying, *I sure have a tough day ahead of me,* or *I know she doesn't love me.*

> The following affirmation technique is a synthesis from many schools of positive thinking. It has worked well for me personally and for my clients. Let's define affirmation as a specific positive thought you create in response to a current need or goal.

> We've heard negative programming thousands of times; now it's important to use our minds for positive results. Once we create a powerful, positive affirmation, we must continue thinking it each day until it becomes a natural part of us. We can't erase the old and familiar, but we can create the new and have a choice in what we think or say to ourselves. At times the old and the new will come into conflict; this must be acknowledged and worked through.

Here is our affirmation exercise:

1. Define your desire (in this case, a relationship desire).
2. Think back to the parental message you needed as a child that could permit or affirm that desire.

3. Write the affirmation fifteen times, always including your name: five times in the first person, five times in the second, and five times in the third. (Example: "I, John, deserve love." "You, John, deserve love." "He, John, deserves love.")
4. Listen for any negative responses or feelings you experience while doing these affirmations; if there are any, write them down.
5. Continue to refine your affirmation so it fits comfortably against the negative responses. When it is as you want it, repeat it fifteen times.
6. Imagine your life as if the affirmation had become reality.
7. Release the thought; let your energy flow into pursuits that will turn it into reality.
8. Live your life as though the affirmation is reality. Create or respond to situations that can help you bring your desire into reality.
9. Move through this exercise several times a day until the desire has become reality or the new belief feels natural to you, or both. You may switch from writing your affirmation to saying or thinking it.

— Brenda Schaeffer

We suggest that you work on an affirmation now. If you would like to work on affirmations about writing, we would like to suggest the following as openers from the work of Larry Block, in his book *Write for Your Life*.

The more I take it easy, the more I accomplish.
You have all the time you need to write successfully.
It's natural for me to write honestly.
You are an endless source of wonderful ideas.

— Larry Block

The writer Mary Kay Rummel looked back through her journal to see her affirmations. She was interested in how they worked, how they changed, and what effect they had on her life. Here are some excerpts from her 1987 journal, with comments from 1988 printed in italics.

TILTING TOWARD THE LIGHT

The summer of 1987 was an important time in my recovering. Old destructive voices were clamoring in my head, trying to take over my life. My family life was unsettled, my job was unsettled and I was feeling very lonely. Each day I wrote affirmations in my journal to counteract the negative voices from my past....I want to share a tool that really did help me change my self talk.

May 6, 1987
I need to write. My pen and notebook keep me on earth, connecting, noticing, listening.

May 7, 1987
I talk to myself. I am in training, retraining myself each day. Each day the old voices speak up. Each day I speak with a new voice. I AM I AM I AM

"Be good."
I AM GOOD.
I AM PERFECT FOR NOW.
"Be beautiful."
I AM BEAUTIFUL AND CREATIVE NOW.

May 10, 1987
I listen to my body now.
What does it say?
It says, "Be centered in the moment.
Trust me. Don't be afraid."

May 11, 1987
This body is all I know.

For me, silencing negative voices means listening to the strong intuitive voice of my own body.

May 14, 1987
I am living creatively in the present, using it productively for myself and others. My senses are turned outward. I perceive all the beauty of the moment from the song of the cardinal that fills my ears to the flash of orioles through the lacy green trees.

You can tell from reading my affirmations that I am trying to change self-talk that is filled with worry, fear about the future and guilt, into self-talk that affirms the beauty and strength of my own self and my trust in a loving Higher Power.

May 17, 1987
I am creating my own time, weaving it like a basket with the moments of my life. To make time is what I do. It is mine. I do what I want with it and I know that what I do is beautiful and healthy.... If I weave it from inside, the filling will take care of itself. I create the basket and it will be filled.

May 20, 1987
Like all of nature, I am tilting toward the light and in the light and power of the universe I blossom....I am walking a green journey.

May 25, 1987
Every person I connect with is a gift, a source of learning and light for me. All the good I need is coming to me right now.

As I change my thoughts about myself, my thoughts about my relationships also change.

May 28, 1987
...I am with myself. I let go of the fear of loneliness and of something happening beyond my control. I bring peace to my relationships.

May 30, 1987
My life becomes the thing I have decided it shall
be. I can remake old decisions. My life is a
beautiful, alive and passionate thing, full of
attunement to the moment....

*Belief in my own goodness, trust in my Higher Power
and the letting go of fear and anxiety are the themes
that I come back to again and again in my affirmations.
Writing them centers me in the present, and during this
summer I found I was more and more able to focus on
the work I wanted to do.*

May 31, 1987
As I begin each task, I put all my worries in a
shoebox, promising to take them out at a later
time....In this way I can work.

November, 1988
*This is not a story. There are no endings. The daily
work of change and recovery goes on and on. I look back
at what I wrote during the summer of 1987 and I see
that I am still affirming the same reality, often writing
the same words. I also see that slowly it is becoming
automatic. Slowly, the way I think about myself and my
life is changing.*

— Mary Kay Rummel

A Place of Peace: Visualizations and Meditations

Making affirmations and making visualizations are two different processes. They entail two different kinds of work. Affirmations deal with abstract statements of belief. They may or
may not give us visual images (pictures) when we write and
say them. Some people report that they have kinesthetic sensations of well-being while in the process of writing affirmations, but these sensations do not necessarily include visual

images. The sounds of the words coming out of our bodies and the flow of writing across the paper change the tapes we carry around in our minds.

But visualization does center pictures in our minds. When we make a new visualization, we make new pictures for our minds to take the place of dismal, gloomy pictures. Sometimes we may give our minds pictures for what we think is a pictureless outlook. Our minds seem blank of hope. Pictures give hope.

We are going to ask that you write a visualization, but first we want to clarify the terms that go with visualizations, for they have some overlapping territory. The terms we'll discuss are:

- Creative Visualization
- Guided Imagery
- Meditation

Creative Visualization

Let's think for a minute about the words *creative* and *visualization*. *To visualize* means to see. *Creative* means to make new, to make out of nothing. Creative visualizations are creations that we make to see another reality, a reality that could exist in our lives, if we let it.

Creative visualizations are imaginary trips to safe, peaceful places. The deep woods with a warm, sunny meadow. An ocean shore with tide pools and sand. The jungle with waterfalls and pools and lush foliage. The center of the earth, with its molten lava, rising up with new energy to the air. Each trip involves a journey to a special place and a time for relaxation at the end of the journey, a time to be at one with nature.

Guided Imagery

When someone else takes us on this journey, we call the process *guided imagery*. The word *image* is nothing more than the French word for *picture*. When we go on a guided imagery trip, a guide is showing us pictures of another reality. We might recall that movies used to be called "picture shows."

Some people who are talented at imagining may conduct this process for others without writing. As they say the words out loud, they lead us toward the special imagery place, and they remember what they see along the way.

But writing our own visualizations can capture the journey so that if we go away from it for a long period of time, we will be able to come back to it. We can also give it to other people when it is written down. Let us turn now to one way of writing a visualization.

Visualization and Imagery Give Us a Place of Meditation

The purpose of having an imaginary place is to create a state of mind receptive to meditation. The purpose of meditation is to quiet the mind. The process of going to the place is one form of meditation. Of course, there are other kinds of meditation. Lying down on the bed and letting our minds go blank is the easiest. Some people who practice yoga concentrate on the flame of a candle. Other people practice other forms of meditation. It is important to discover what works for you.

Later in this chapter, we will discuss writing other kinds of meditations, but for now we are going to look at creative visualization as a way to practice meditation.

People in Twelve Step programs use a variety of forms of meditation. Step Eleven states that the purpose for prayer and meditation is "to improve our conscious contact with God." There are many choices available for prayer and meditation. The ideas we are presenting in this chapter have been used by some people in the program for Step Eleven. By no means are these the only choices, but these choices are appealing to people who like to write.

Writing about Our Querencia: A Creative Visualization

Querencia is a Spanish word that refers to the "most-loved place, the place to which one returns for healing of the spirit."

Sit quietly and get in touch with all the places on earth that you love. Which place gives you the greatest feeling of peace?

You might also think of paintings that give you a sense of peace. Often, the image of a scene in a painting stays with us throughout our lifetime. Even though we may have never visited the place in the painting, there is something about it that calls us. It is odd that we can feel at home with a place we've never been, but it happens. If you feel stuck, we suggest that you take an afternoon and visit an art museum. Let yourself wander aimlessly. You will probably find one picture that draws you in.

Once you've thought of a place, real or painted, try writing, according to the following directions. (Remember, too, that the techniques we use to describe an imaginary place are the same techniques we use to describe a real place — the five senses, and details — the eye of the camera.)

Querencia

Start writing as if you were talking to someone who can't see your place, who has never been there.

Pretend you're walking toward your place. You are approaching it slowly, taking in the whole world around it — horizon, sky, vista.

Describe the wholeness of what you see. The landscape. Tell about the colors and shapes, the cast of light. As you are writing, discover the time of day. There are differences in a place depending on the time of day. Daybreak, noon, twilight, midnight. What is your favorite time to be here?

Now listen for the sounds. You may have to listen a long time, if you are listening back thirty years to your childhood. Don't worry, the sounds are still there. Crickets, rivers, music, baseball on the radio.

As you enter your place, describe any paths, roads, secret trails.

Now be in your place. Just be there and tell what is around you. Are you cold? Relaxed? Active? Use all five senses. What can you smell? Leaves? Grass?

You may be sitting and dozing, but you may want to be more active. What are you doing? Fishing? Swimming? Riding horseback?

Say to yourself, *It's good to be here.* What's good about it? Let yourself feel the goodness and find words for it.

Stay in this place as long as you want. Let your mind drift. Write down some of your drifting thoughts, observations, feelings.

When it is time to go, say good-bye to your *Querencia.* Write a brief farewell. Show appreciation for what you have received.

There is much to feel gratitude for. The special places on earth are gifts we don't always stop to say thank-you for. *Thank you, lake. Thank you, trails.* This may sound childish, but it does release a wide open channel of love for the world.

Once you have written a visualization like this one, there are several ways to use it.

You may write it, know it, close your eyes and say it to yourself. You may make a tape of it, and play it for yourself when you need some deep quiet time. Or you may ask a friend to read it to you. It is wonderful to hear a friend read your writing. It is nurturing to you and to your friendship.

There are many books that have visualizations and guided imagery you can use. Some of these are *Creative Visualization* by Shakti Gawain, *Mother Wit: A Feminist Guide to Psychic Development,* by Diane Mariechild, *The Inner Dance,* also by Diane Mariechild, and *The Centering Book: Awareness Activities for Children, Parents, and Teachers,* by Gay Hendricks and Russel Wills. This last book is good if you have young children. In it you can learn how to tell each other your dreams first thing in the morning.

Other Writing Ideas for Your Own Meditations

If you tried writing about your *Querencia,* you will have found a new spiritual place. You might want to write more pieces like this. You could ramble to other places; this time you might go inside a favorite house. You could also set out on a new journey to discover a new *Querencia* within the year. You could walk to new places and look for a new peaceful place. Every recovery program can benefit from time out of doors.

Some people have used as a centering image the painting they loved as a child, or a drawing in a book they read as a child. Writing about pictures you've drawn yourself is also helpful. We will discuss drawing and writing in the last chapter of the book.

In addition to writing about peaceful images, you may want to explore writing your own "Thought for the Day," similar to the short meditations that are published by some religious and Twelve Step publishers. Why not write your own, specially tailored to your continuing concerns and obsessions? We're not suggesting that you write 365 daily meditations. Maybe one or two. You might write a meditation that sums up where you are on your spiritual journey now, reminding you of what you want to know for this day.

A "Thought for the Day" has its own form, just as a poem or story. It is short, thought-provoking, reflective. To start, you might look through the books of your favorite writers. Write down a few quotes that catch your eye. (Or maybe you've already been collecting favorite quotes in your journal.) Then choose one of the quotes to work with today. Ask yourself the following questions about it. What does this remind me of from my life? A memory? A feeling? A fleeting thought I had on the freeway yesterday?

For example, one person picked a quote from Nor Hall.

Withdrawal is a preparation for emergence.

This quote seems full of mystery. It gives validation for the times in our lives when we can't manage to be energetic. It gives us permission to take time for solitude. The person who picked this quote tried to think of an anecdote that somehow exemplified the statement.

A man lost his family in a car accident and wanted to be alone for a while, but he worried whether he was doing the right thing. Then one day a friend told him that when pine cones fall off the Lodge Pole Pine trees, they are sealed shut so the seeds inside can't get out. The pine cones lie on the forest floor — sometimes for decades — until a forest fire sweeps through. Heat from the fire melts the seal and the seeds fall out and finally grow, and that's why the Lodge Pole Pine is called a *fire origin species.*

The man felt good about himself when he heard the story. *Fire origin species* is a good name for people who've been burned by life and find new growth as a result.

You don't need to write any more than a couple of paragraphs. You may do some writing on automatic pilot and then choose your favorite two paragraphs to go with the quote. Remember, a "Thought for the Day" is short, to the point.

After you're done writing, look over what you have written and think about what conclusions you can draw. Is there a message? Is there a hope for a certain quality of life? See if you can distill a thought.

Some meditations end with a summary statement or affirmation. Others end with a question, or an open-ended, fill-in-the-blank for the reader. The meditation from the book *Today's Gift,* concludes with this question: *How have I grown because of pain and difficulty?*

Prayers

Writing prayers may not seem like writing. But the process of living and breathing and writing and praying are intertwined and often merged. Living a life of prayer implies living a life open to spiritual consciousness.

Some people say, "The desire to pray is prayer itself." And, maybe, the desire to write a prayer is a prayer itself.

Even when we accept this attitude of praying, which comes from many spiritual traditions, there are times when we want to say and write specific words for specific situations, even if only to admit, "I don't have the slightest idea what to do next." All spiritual traditions offer forms for prayers.

Many people in the Twelve Step programs say that prayer is the process of asking, and meditation is the process of listening for the answer. You may wonder why we then discussed meditation first in this chapter. What we have noticed in our own journeys is that we had to learn to sit still and listen before we had any idea what it was we wanted to ask for. So for us, learning to quiet the mind was both meditation and prayer.

Before talking about writing prayers, it is important to talk for a moment about specific barriers people have to making their own prayers. What holds us back?

Four Barriers to a Natural Response

1. *Guilt over previous desperate pleas.* This is the plea of, "God, get me out of this one and I'll never do it again." This guilt deserves to go to the big pit along with all our other guilts.
2. *Confusion about our definition of God.* It is possible to pray without having a conscious definition of God. People do it all the time. It is possible to pray without any sense of whom or what we're praying to. Maybe even wanting a definition is part of our linear thinking which is not all that helpful. But we'll put a definition in here anyway, from the book *Original Blessing,* by Matthew Fox. Fox quotes Jewish scholar, Ronald Miller, who says that in the Old Testament, "God is the ultimate with." This sense of with-ness is enough of a definition for many people: Jews, agnostics, pagans, and Christians.

In writing about spiritual traditions from Africa, Louisah Teish writes about this sense of with-ness:

African spirituality says that getting up in the morning is worship, cooking your meals is worship, washing your body is worship, working in your garden is worship, sweeping your floor is worship, making love is an act of worship. Worship is every act done with integrity and love and the understanding that it is connected to the overall scheme of Nature. The tradition teaches the real dynamics of power and to trust that your own head, your own ovary, your own crown chakra is connected to the big holy picture of God and Nature.

— Louisah Teish

3. *Weariness over all the pain in the world.* The Eleventh Step is a step of liberation from the endless lists of pain in the world. The Eleventh Step is a permission-giving step. Each person doesn't have to take on all the world's burdens. It says: "...praying only for knowledge of God's will for us and the power to carry that out."

This Step lifts the weariness and dread that come from thinking prayer means solving all the world's problems. In fact, it points to a certain codependent and grandiose view of prayer. Prayer is much simpler. The most simple prayer is, "What is my assignment for today, oh, *You-who-are-there?*"

4. *Guilt over a sloppy spiritual program.* Put this guilt the same place you put the guilt in number 1. And get on with it.

Writing a Prayer Just for Today

Now, we can get back to writing prayers. Certain words are typical of prayers, chants, and rituals, regardless of the spiritual group they come from. Some of these words are: *let, may, please, manifest,* and *love.* To start writing a prayer, focus on the primary spiritual state you desire to be in today. Peacefulness, energy. Then try the following formula as your opening prayer for the day. You can set this up in your journal or in a separate notebook.

1. Think of how you'd care to address your God. The opening of the prayer can be called the address, or the invocation. You might say, "Dear God or Goddess." We like "Oh, Gracious One."

   Address: _____

2. The body of the prayer is like the body of the letter, holding the bulk of meaning. Remember, your focus in this prayer is to ask for the spiritual state you desire to be in today, in accordance with the good of all and God's will.

   Body: Let me be _____ today.
   Open my heart to _____.
   Open my mind to _____.
   May _____ be manifest in the world.

3. Ask for God's will to be expressed to you. Think of your own unique way of asking for this.

   God's Will: I ask _____.

4. No prayer would be complete without an expression of gratitude and thanksgiving. This opens us to feeling the love that already exists for us in the world. Consider what you are thankful for today.

   Thanks: I carry in my mind's eye the vision of my gifts, and I thank You for all my blessings:
   _____ (list blessings).

5. The closing of a prayer is a way of giving yourself a benediction and asking for the manifestation of the words in the prayer. You can choose a traditional ending, "Amen," "Let the blessings be," or you can make up a new one. That is up to you.

   Close: _____.

When people work on prayers, they start out with a short model, like the one above, and then add on. Then they read other ideas, and add special paragraphs for individual concerns.

Using Our Backgrounds in Writing Prayers

Some people grew up in a home that didn't practice any spiritual tradition. But most people have some connection to some religious tradition. These traditions can be a resource for us as adults, even if we no longer follow all the practices of our parents. Often we remember the form and rhythm of a childhood ritual. We can express and reclaim this heritage in our writing. We can adapt the form of a prayer to include the concerns we have about our present adult lives. For example, Pat Panagoulias, a member of the Chippewa people, White Earth Reservation, Minnesota, invoked ancient Grandmother Moon to express her concerns about addiction. The prayer is published in *Drink the Winds, Let the Waters Flow Free. . .*

If you have a religious background, take some time now to reflect on how any part of this background could give you an image to use in writing a prayer. Where in the world does the spirit of God manifest God's self to you? In the moon? In the wind? Try writing about your recovery with one image from your childhood religion.

Because this book's focus is writing, we want to share with you a longer prayer that was written by a writer. Many writers use affirmations and prayers to work through the fears that can block creativity. This prayer was written and compiled from other sources by Jill Breckenridge.

PRAYER ASKING FOR BLESSING ON CREATIVE WORK

(address of your choosing),

At this moment and for all eternity, I offer you my heart, mind, body, and spirit, dedicating to you whatever work you would do through me.

Help me be unerringly true to the inner voice — let it surprise me with truths I didn't know I knew. Help me let go of the ground of rigid rationality for the sake of the creative intuitive leap. As my creative genius is released, help me to set aside my little ego and be obedient to the risk and to the work.

May I live a constant prayer, and may faith in your plan for me defeat all fear in the knowledge that my task is merely to do the work at hand. Let my faith be supported by patience, since patience accompanies all deep love. During times when the work is difficult, let me know you will never give me a job for which I am not prepared.

Hone the edge of my discipline so that I may cut through any resistance, remembering that a disciple is one who is allured and attracted to her work. Let me be brave enough to forge the creative fire which turns that which is old into the new.

Let me die to self and live inspired in the work I have been given to do, knowing that for now and for all time, all shall be well, and all shall be well, and all manner of things shall be well. Thy will be done. Amen.

— Jill Breckenridge

Writing a Blessing for Your Creative Work

Reflect on the prayer written by Jill Breckenridge and ask what you most need to be able to do your work in a centered and trusting manner. You might make a list of the qualities that you know are beneficial to you. Then start a prayer, and use some of the following words in connection with the qualities that you desire: *I offer, I dedicate, Help me, May I, Let my faith, Let me know, Let me be relaxed enough to* _____.

May you find your own benediction in this writing. And may you all come to feel the blessing of the words: *a diamond must be broken before it can shine.*

CHAPTER 6

Walking in Someone Else's Shoes: Altered Points of View

...the bright stranger, the foreign self.
— Ralph Waldo Emerson

I am sensible to a certain doubleness by which
I stand as remote from myself as from another.
— Henry David Thoreau

We've often heard people quip, "If you were in my shoes, you'd understand," or "I'd sure hate to be in his shoes." This metaphor suggests that to understand other people you need to be in their shoes, in their skin, and to have their hearts and souls to grasp their situation. In writing, the altered point of view contributes to strengthening an individual's ability to empathize. It also opens the door to aspects of our own personalities we may not be conscious of. In this way we learn to empathize with ourselves as well.

Professional writers and Gestalt therapists often work with the altered point of view. To do this, you pretend to be someone you're not, a relative or the tall man wearing a straw hat in your dream. You write what he has to say, even though he may have remained silent in the dream. Or you write about yourself in the third person. This is a way of using Gestalt therapy in writing and journals.

Altered point of view is a good way to get at feelings, thoughts, or experiences that we can't get to any other way. Changing a first person statement like "I didn't know what to say to her" to "He didn't know what to say to her" can provide just enough detachment and distance that allows you to grasp the situation more fully.

The writing exercises in this chapter are aimed at getting us into another person's shoes in order to grow and live more compassionately. In addition, exercises here will help us to detach from ourselves in order to find other alternatives and open us up to different feelings, perspectives, and thoughts.

Novelists often have to express the opposing views of characters and this may require them to express ideas that normally might abhor them. Think of all the novels you read, even the television programs, that include murder and violence. These characters and scenes may represent the very worst in life. It's hard to even imagine what a murderer might be thinking, let alone even want to. Yet script writers and novelists must in order to create the dramas they do. Fortunately, diarists and writers rarely ever have to stretch their imaginations to such violent extremes. Still, for plenty of us, taking the altered point of view takes guts and courage. For those who come from severely dysfunctional families or have experienced excessive abuse in marriages, taking the altered point of view can be threatening and emotional.

Writing from the perspectives of our parents and siblings allows us to experience the past in a unique way. As an adult, we can go back to our childhood and write from the child's point of view, that is, the child we were. We can relive experiences. This time, the child who was silent can speak. The child can boldly gesture when he or she may have actually remained curled up in bed. We can write what we didn't say to our mothers or fathers when they, for example, disappointed us on Christmas Eve by getting drunk at our grandparents' house.

This kind of writing helps integrate old feelings with new thoughts and views.

Of course, the viewpoints we explore come out of ourselves. The voices may sound real enough, but still the voices are one voice. Ours! Experimenting with altered points of view allows us to experience the angles of the many-faceted jewel called the Self.

Talking to Old Friends

Let's start with a simple conversation, a dialogue with an old friend. Let's say this friend has either died or moved away. If you have had someone like this in your life, use the individual's name. For example, we'll select a man in his mid-thirties named Greg. You grew up with this man, attended grade school together, rode your bikes on long Saturday afternoon trips, and even went to the same high school. During your college years, the two of you took separate paths. Ten years later, you return home for a brief visit. You renewed your relationship, talked about "old times."

You leave again. In less than two years, you hear he died of a heart attack.

Get a picture of him in your mind. Get a feeling of his presence, imagine him sitting in a chair across from you, and begin writing a simple dialogue. It's important to write this out. Don't let your mind get ahead of you. Let yourself have a genuine dialogue, where neither one nor the other monopolizes the conversation. Start with a simple statement.

Writer: You look good, Greg. It's been so long.
Greg: Yes, it has. A long, long time.
Writer: I've often thought of you. Do you remember the time when we were kids and smoked a cigarette behind those pine trees at the corner of Saybrook and East 136th Street?

Greg:	Oh, yes, my God we were scared. Every time a car drove by we thought it was your father coming home for lunch.
Writer:	I stopped smoking last year.
Greg:	I know that. You're mad at me now, aren't you?
Writer:	Well, a little I guess. I didn't think I was. But you were warned. Your mother told me years after you died that you were warned by the doctor to stop smoking. He said your heart was weak.
Greg:	And did you do all the things the doctors, the teachers, and your parents told you to do?
Writer:	Of course not. But still I'm angry. And besides that, I asked you before I left to come and visit me in Ohio, but you never did. And you didn't answer my letters...

In this unfinished dialogue, we read that the writer is angry at his best friend who died. The writer may be surprised at learning about his anger. Had the dialogue continued, he may have learned more. This is a simple example of how you might begin. Now, try your own dialogue and see what you might discover about yourself or the other person.

Dreams and Writing

This writing exercise requires three steps and involves dreams and the altered point of view. First, select a particular dream you can vividly recall. Pick one that you haven't discussed with a therapist or one that doesn't seem self-explanatory. Select a dream that slightly puzzles you. It may seem like an odd dream, a dream with some peculiarities. Write the dream out now and record only its description. Don't try to analyze it, but simply describe or "show" it.

Second, select a particular aspect of the dream that most interests you. Select one of its characters. Maybe a chair appeared in your dream that still impresses you because of the brightness of its color. You have never seen a red so bright and so rich before. Possibly a tall man wearing a hat did appear in your dream. Select him.

Third, engage this person (or object) in a dialogue. Of course you'll have to step into his or her shoes and put the appropriate words in the person's mouth until you have an identity separate from yours. We often suggest to our students that they first close their eyes and try to get a picture of the person or object (it could even be a peculiar smell or aroma) in their minds in order to heighten the sense of separation from the person or thing. Once you've done this, begin writing a dialogue with that person or object. Yes, even objects can talk in this exercise!

We've selected a person for this example. Try to imagine a boy about twelve who appears in your dream wearing only a toga. He is walking behind you down a very busy street in Chicago, although no particular sign said the city was Chicago. It's just something you know. In your dream the boy says nothing. He appears briefly and doesn't otherwise carry a significant place in your dream. Still, you wonder about him and have a curious sense of him. Your dialogue could begin like this.

Writer: Who are you?
Boy: (Remains silent, but stoops to pick up a rock.)
Writer: What's that? A rock, a pebble? Why? You are so intriguing. Please, tell me, who are you?
Boy: I came from India long ago and have been lost. You remind me of my father. Only my father never asked me so many questions.
Writer: But you're in my dream. If you got lost in Chicago, why are you in my dream, and now here in my house, talking?

Boy: I can walk in and out of life and visit people's
         dreams and reappear in daylight, real life
         as you think of it. I am looking for my
         father and I've come to you because you
         know something about Tibet.
Writer: Me! Oh, no. You're wrong. I've never visited
         Tibet or any country in Asia. Honestly, this
         is crazy. I don't even meditate.
Boy: No, listen. Tibet is cold, infinite and...
Writer: I'm losing you.
Boy: It doesn't matter. I'll visit you again. I will
         wear a different costume, one that you'll
         understand. Maybe I'll be older. We'll talk
         for a long time now that you've contacted
         me. I know you think I'm a wise boy,
         someone who will help you. But I'm not.
         I'm only a boy. I'm in you, your dreams,
         I'm a child who needs you.

We see from this example that the boy, who originally played an incidental role in the person's dream, has a significant relationship with the dreamer or writer. Also, the writer has separated himself from the boy and created an authentic dialogue. We don't know yet if the writer accepts the idea. There's a sense at the end of this conversation that the boy is the dreamer's inner child, though the boy won't actually say so. In the next exercise, we will introduce an additional approach that can be taken to unravel our dreams. We use another writing method to see how the writer can learn more about the boy.

More Dream Writing

Let's go back to the original dream you recorded and described early in this exercise. We'll take four different steps of an additional method to use in understanding dreams.

First, write down three questions you have about your dream.

Don't make the questions rhetorical, that is, questions you already know the answers to. Your questions should be genuinely challenging, questions you truly want answered. List three of them now.

Second, select the question that concerns you the most. A question you hear no answer to. Circle it.

Third, imagine for a moment that there is in fact a Dream Interpreter, an Oracle like the one in Delphi, Greece, who could answer questions and interpret dreams for the citizens of ancient Greece. This Dream Interpreter could be from any culture, any era, of any gender. Describe this Dream Interpreter in a paragraph or two. Your description will lend credibility to this exercise.

Finally, prepare to have a dialogue with your Dream Interpreter. Remember, the Dream Interpreter is another person or object, different from you, and the resulting conversation will come accordingly. Start the dialogue with the question you circled earlier.

For our example we will return to the writer with the dream of the boy in the earlier dialogue. If you find this exercise difficult because your Dream Interpreter doesn't seem real enough to you yet, then start with another challenge.

Writer:	Really, now, are you the Dream Interpreter?
Dream Interpreter:	I thought you were instructed not to ask rhetorical questions, questions you know the answers to.
Writer:	So, you aren't real. This is just another one of those crazy writing exercises that instructors concoct.
Dream Interpreter:	If you want it to be.
Writer:	All right, I'll bite. Tell me then the answer to this question. A boy appeared in my dream

	wearing a toga and said he was looking for his father and I want to know...
Dream Interpreter:	I know what you want to know. You are his father, only you haven't recognized that yet. The boy won't come out and say so because you'll treat him the same way you treated me in the beginning. With disbelief, aloofness, and disdain.
Writer:	Well, it's too damn easy for me to be the father's boy. I mean really, this comes straight out of a psychology 101 class where the "child in you"...you know how it goes. Well, say something.
Dream Interpreter:	You forgot the question you wanted answered.
Writer:	All right tell me. Where is his real father?
Dream Interpreter:	Lost. If you calm down, if you let your mind drift into the moonlight, if you let your doubt be a pebble thrown into a lake, dissolving in the cold water, if you let me rest and sit down on the edge of your bed, I will tell you.
Writer:	All right, sit down. I'm serious now. Tell me.
Dream Interpreter:	Do you remember where the boy comes from?

Writer:	Yes, from Tibet, I think. Some place far, cold, and infinite, he said.
Dream Interpreter:	That's right. And do you remember where I come from?
Writer:	Is this a quiz show? I'm sorry. Yes, I remember.
Dream Interpreter:	Yes. The boy and I both come from afar, from foreign countries. This is where you keep us. Far away. And it is cold, and we are infinite. It was the boy who created the sense of Chicago in you, a place more familiar than Tibet in order to bring him closer to you. We are your voice. Only you keep us far away.
Writer:	Yes, I see. I am the boy. Am I you, the Dream Interpreter? Yes, of course I am.
Dream Interpreter:	This is partly true. But you are more than the boy and I. You have other unheard voices and people you have not called upon or listened to. But this is enough for now.

In this dialogue, the writer finally reaches some understanding of who the boy is, as well as who the Dream Interpreter is. This writer acquires the significant insight that he has ignored his inner child, who feels lost or abandoned.

Of course, you create the Dream Interpreter, and the dialogue is with yourself. It's a "voice" that we rarely express or listen to. Writing allows us to tap into our resources and learn that we have many voices inside that allow us deeper insights and perspectives.

Through this exercise, you will discover you have a variety of voices, and that they need to be heard. You need to hear them. You need to give them a chance to speak. In dysfunctional families, there is only one voice that talks and gets heard, and that voice is the voice of the bottle, the voice of the drug, the addiction — the obsession that preoccupies the entire family. These exercises will lead you to discover the many voices you truly have, the voices that may have gone unheard for a long time.

Talking to Yourself

We often excuse our mumbling to people by saying, "Oh, I'm sorry, I was just talking to myself." People often quip, "Well, as long as you're not answering yourself." This jokingly refers to the fact that if you're answering your own questions you might not be mentally sound. In this section, you will answer your own questions. You will write in two voices, one asking questions, and the other answering. This is similar to the altered points of view we practiced with dreams earlier in this chapter. Only here, the dialogue will be more direct.

If you recall, in the chapter on descriptive writing, you were asked to write descriptions of feelings as people. Now, we will ask you to engage the feelings you describe in a dialogue. This exercise is similar to the dialogue we described with the Dream Interpreter. You simply use what you wrote earlier. You record a simple conversation with a particular feeling. For example, let's say you've already described fear as man in his seventies, dressed in polyester pants and shirt. He is sitting in a park on a bench, tossing bits of bread to pigeons that swarm around his feet. He is always looking over his shoulder, as if expecting someone. You may begin your dialogue with fear in this manner.

Writer: Why are you always looking over your shoulder?

Fear: You know why. You never know who might
come up suddenly behind you.

Writer: Yeah, but somehow you always get in my
way and cause me a great deal of dis-
comfort.

Fear: I'm minding my own business. Ignore me.

Writer: Well, that's just it. I can't ignore you. Why
just yesterday you kept me from speaking
my mind at our annual board meeting.

Fear: I didn't do that. I was simply warning you
that your views with the board are very
controversial and they may ask you to resign.
You are the one who chose not to talk.

Writer: You made me afraid to talk.

Fear: No, I simply make you aware of what could
go wrong. I'm not evil. You don't have to
let my fear keep you from doing what you
want....

At this point in the dialogue, the writer has come to an interesting revelation about his fear. The antagonism the writer
first felt toward fear has lessened, and fear takes on a less
threatening, almost wise demeanor. Remember, the voice of
fear in the previous dialogue is actually the writer's voice.
Through dialogue and the altered point of view, the writer has
become more conscious of his other views and inner voices.
This is the magic of the altered point of view. We learn to tap
into our inner reservoir of resources. We can reach perspectives and views that were actually in us all along.

Select a feeling you've already described as a person and have
your own dialogue with it.

This exercise may help you "get in touch" with your feelings.
Early recovery especially requires this new relatedness to your
feelings. On the other hand, getting in touch with your feelings isn't an end-all or cure-all. Many people think that getting

in touch with feelings will resolve their conflicts. But life is not so simple. Getting in touch with feelings puts us in contact with "bad" feelings as well as good feelings. For this reason, a person may experience more anger and shame in a recovery program than in the days of codependency or chemical dependency. When dependencies are active, people often don't have feelings; rather, feelings have them.

More Dialogues

Getting in touch with *what we think* is equally important. Thoughts often create feelings. We respond emotionally to what we think.

We can extend the inner dialogue exercises to include writing imaginary conversations with concepts, such as the censor, the critic, the conscience, the soul, the child in us, our future selves. Through this method, we can integrate our thoughts and feelings and respond maturely.

To do this next exercise, select a particular concept or thought you wish to talk with. As you did earlier with feelings, describe in a paragraph or two this concept, giving it flesh and blood, clothes, a face, a location. Then, apply what you learned about writing dialogue to the concept.

We've included here an example of a poet having a dialogue with her inner critic.

Me: Here's some poems I've just written. Would you read them and tell me what you think?

Critic: Hmm, hmm. Yes, well, you certainly do write a lot, don't you? And perhaps at times you go on too long. Do you ever revise your poems?

Me: Well yes, I do. But never seriously. Mostly just a little....

Critic: What do you mean "just a little"?

Me: Well, I read them at a reading, and then I can tell where they don't sound like ordinary speech.

Critic: Like ordinary speech? You're trying to make your poems sound like *ordinary* speech?

Me: Well, yes. You know, like how people really talk....

Critic: Why in the world would you want to do that?

Me: I'm not sure. Well, yes I am. I do know why. That is, I think I know why. I want to be sure everybody understands my poems.

Critic: Everybody? You want everybody to understand your poems? Is that what you think poems are for? Don't you think perhaps poems should be a special kind of language that forces people to think hard? Don't you think poetry should concern itself with deep images that people, that is ordinary people, cannot be expected to get or understand as you put it — or at least not until they've put a great deal of effort into it. Do you want your poems to be EASY READING?

Me: Not exactly. No, of course not. I don't want to be considered easy. Maybe in one way I do want to be easy. I don't want people to turn away and not read my poems because they've got some notion that poetry is too hard, or even too good for them — in the sense of too highfalutin or elevated — too removed from their daily life. I want my poems to be clear, maybe, that's what I'm really saying. Yes, that's it. I want to be clear. (I'm sick of writing all this now. I'm suddenly resentful that I even am here and forced into writing this. I don't want to do it anymore and, what's more, I won't. My eyes aren't too good, anyhow, what with having to wear these stupid glasses because I had to give my other glasses to Mike because he broke his and he asked me where were all the old pairs of his glasses that I borrowed and never returned and of course I had to say I don't know where they are and out of fairness I simply had to give him mine.)

We see in the last section of dialogue the poet exclaims, "Yes, that's it." Here, she finally comes to affirm and establish what she wants for her poetry. Clarity. Yet, her inner critic earlier nagged and reproached her for lack of "poetic" language. We see how her ideas of clarity and poetics had not been integrated and caused her conflict. This dialogue helps her understand the subsequent tension she might feel. It's also amusing to note her tangent at the end when she tires of her dialogue with the inner critic.

Try this exercise and it may help clarify your own conflicts. You don't have to resolve them. Sometimes just writing out the conversation and observing the relationship between the inner critic or concept and yourself is helpful.

Using a Narrator

When we say *narrator*, we mean the person or voice that tells the story who may or may not be actually in the story. The point of view can give us a chance to tell a story from inside the consciousness of all the characters. In this case, the narrative or omniscient voice is all-knowing. The writer remains behind the scenes knowing what all the characters are thinking, feeling, and doing. Narrative voice offers an altered point of view that we can use in writing.

When we discussed journal writing, we asked you to list three secrets and describe them in detail. If you found that exercise difficult or emotional, you might use an altered point of view, specifically in the third person, narrative voice.

One student, Diedre C., gives an example of how helpful the narrative voice can be when the material is extremely shameful or difficult to express. At first, she simply wouldn't write about one of the secrets she listed on her paper. Even though she was in her forties, one childhood event still caused too much shame for her to write about it. After a great deal of encouragement, she wrote out her secret — that as a child she had stolen money from her father's desk drawer — in a short poem. Although the poem had strong feeling, it was lacking detail. In fact, the secret remained a secret in the poem. A reader of this poem would suspect the author had stolen some money once, yet the shame and remorse the author conveyed in the poem seemed puzzling, out of proportion to the event. She was excessively cruel to herself in the poem in light of the simple act of theft which, like lying, everyone has committed at least once. This was the first draft of her secret.

> Small hands reaching in my father's desk stealing coins I didn't really want. Body trembles as I shut the drawer feeling like a strange intruder. Running out to spend the coins that hurt my hands if I hold on to them for very long. Please help me Daddy, make me stop. I'm so afraid you'll leave me if you see me as I really am and know the things these small hands do. Tell me you'll love me even if I'm bad.
>
> — Diedre C.

She said she couldn't admit entirely to the secret in the poem. But she confessed that the single incident of theft was actually compulsive, weekly stealing. She hadn't stolen just once, but more times than she could keep track of. She recalled wanting to get caught each time she stole a few coins. Others were blamed for it. For over twenty years, she hid this past from others, keeping this experience hidden in her shame. She agreed to rewrite it, adding more detail.

Even after her revision, however, the poem seemed impersonal and abstract. She just couldn't bring herself to tell. When it was suggested she use a fictional third person narrative voice, her writing took off like a rocket. Her prose and details sparked new energy. This was her answer. She had finally found a voice that helped her detach herself from the experience and write more compassionately and richly. The narrative voice removed her just enough from the experience to write about it. In addition, she put a creative twist at the beginning of the story, using the opposite sex. The opening scene began like this.

Matt peered around his bedroom door to make sure no one was home before going to his father's desk. Walking almost on the toes of his high topped tennis shoes, he crossed the few feet from his bedroom to the dining room and opened the top drawer where his dad kept the money from his insurance customers' premiums. He reached his chubby fingers past the pens and paper clips, over his dad's prayer book, to the metal box where the coins were kept to make change when someone paid in cash. Matt felt the sweat dripping down his face as he touched the box. He stopped with his hand there, and thought about leaving the box in the drawer this time. Instead he took out the box, opened it, and took the nickles and quarters and dimes. He thought, "I'll only take enough to fill one hand" and stuffed the coins quickly into the pocket of his tight jeans. Matt put the box back. . . . He almost wished his dad would spring into the room and catch him and make him stop doing this. But he knew they were out. His mom had told him. . .they were taking his little sister and going for a drive and an ice cream cone, and did he want to come along, too. Matt knew she didn't really want him to come because she was always nagging him about losing weight, but he really would have liked a cone....

— Diedre C.

Later, in the story we find out that Matt takes the money he had stolen and goes to the store to buy "a Hershey bar, a Baby Ruth bar, a small package of peanut M & M's and a Butterfinger bar. . ." Yet outside the candy store, he "threw the M & M's one at a time at the tree in front of the store. . . .He never was able to eat any of the stuff he bought with the stolen coins."

Such an improvement in her writing! There's so much more texture and depth to this writing. Matt, a male alter-ego, allows her to explore her own secret experience in lavish detail and complexity. Not only does she or Matt steal, but we learn he had a serious weight problem that further increases his shame. Something had to "click" for this student. The writing shows the magic that took place inside her.

This is an example of how well the third person narrative voice can help you detach from intense feelings such as shame, guilt, anger, or fear that can constrict the flow of your writing. It also shows that this student works better with fiction than with direct representation of her life. Some people need to write fiction or in a narrative voice to express their deepest feelings.

Go back to that list of three secrets you dealt with in the chapter about journal writing and try writing it out in the third person. Even if you've already written it out in the first person, "I," try the narrative voice. Write about yourself as if you were another person, a "he" or "she" in a story. Although this exercise may seem a little odd at first, it's very simple to do. You can start with "It was a fall evening. The young woman, in her twenties, had just arrived at a friend's house. . ."

You might find yourself wanting to elaborate on events prior to the secret experience. That's fine. Allow yourself to fictionalize a little. Imagine what the weather was that day, and have your character dress accordingly. Give him or her a name, a name different from yours.

"But I really don't know what the weather was like that day. It was so long ago," you might say. That's all right. Just make it up; let it be part of that experience because, in fact, it was, only you don't recall. Using the third person narrative voice gives you a certain liberty. Take advantage of it. You'll find that these details will lend more credibility to the experience and make its reality all the more clear to you.

If you are working a Twelve Step program, this can be an extremely valuable asset to explore your past. A third person narrative can distance you enough from the experience to allow you more objectivity. Having written these experiences out, some people find the Fifth Step much easier and less anxiety-provoking. The Fifth Step says:

> Admitted to God, to ourselves, and to another human
> being the exact nature of our wrongs.

The third person voice allows two people, the narrator and the protagonist, to exist at the same time. It's the favorite voice of fiction writers and many poets.

Aside from using this technique for secrets, it can be used on any subject. Here's an example of a poem using the third person or narrative voice. It's written by a Native American woman named Sharon Day.

THE CHARTINGS

> She had been sober for two years
> When she came across the chartings.
> They were packed neatly away in a trunk
> bound by the hard black/blue covers provided by
> the treatment centers she had frequented.
>
> The chartings were her daily records of feelings:
> an account shared with counselors, prescribed
> by each treatment center as part of the program.

She opened the first packet and began to read.
The writing itself was difficult to make out,
it was scrawled and barely legible —
the counselor's remarks were made in red and
                                        contrasted sharply.

As she read she was overwhelmed with sadness
for the woman who appeared so confused,
so alone and feeling so much pain.

She stopped reading after the first packet
unable to continue, and she wept
for the person she had been
only two short years ago.

— Sharon Day

This poem is an example of how the third person narrative can work for you. When you write this way, you can see how far you've come in your recovery. The poem doesn't have any complex imagery; it shows the power of simple description and understatement.

Altered Point of View and the Tenth Step

You might try this voice with less emotionally charged topics, such as when, in your journal, you write your Tenth Step. Rather than list what went well and what went wrong, you might use the narrative voice and write a short description of your day.

Robert sat down at the end of the day in his favorite chair which allowed him to look out the window to his neighbor's garden. He thought about the altercation he had with his boss. His boss had wanted him to work overtime and Bob had scheduled dinner with his brother for that evening. He didn't want to disappoint his brother whom he had put off for the last two weeks. Too, he didn't want to disappoint his boss who said,

"Bob, I'd really appreciate an hour or two extra from you tonight." The pressure he felt to work overtime made Bob grip the sides of the chair he was sitting in....

By practicing this kind of writing, you'll get a knack for it. The third person narrative voice may become one of your favorite voices to write in. People who generally use this technique are quick to see "the stories" they live each day. They begin to see their life as a story, a story of sadness and joy, a story of drama and tedium, a story of love and loss.

Ninth Step and First Person Fictional Voice

Another voice that can be equally effective is the first person fictional voice. This voice can be especially helpful in working the Ninth Step.

Made direct amends to such people wherever possible, except when to do so would injure them or others.

There may be amends you wish to make, yet you feel too anxious to do it. Try writing out the amends in an imaginary scene, using the first person, "I."
You could start by simply setting the scene.

I am shopping at a grocery store, pushing my cart down the vegetable aisle. I can't remember whether I planned to have asparagus or broccoli for dinner tonight....

After you created a scene where the amends will take place, introduce the person you wish to make amends to. For example, the above writing could continue like this.

At the end of the aisle, where the bananas rest on a turnstile, I see a man snapping off a batch. I recognize him. It's Jim! And he sees me approaching with my cart. I'm tempted to turn around and head back, but as I reach within a few feet of him, he sets the bananas back on the turnstile and approaches. That Friday evening, two years ago, when I insulted him at the bar by calling him a bureaucratic toy for the executives in his company, still causes me shame. I have to apologize and explain how my addiction then interfered and skewed all my relationships. Jim greets me first....

In this example, the writer is able to "rehearse" the amends she eventually hopes to make. This is only one example of how you might apply the first person voice to the Twelve Steps. See if you can discover other ways to benefit from it.

CHAPTER 7

Sincerely Yours:
Letter Writing

> She...read the letter over again: but there
> were phrases that insisted on being read many
> times, they had a life of their own separate
> from the others.
> — Katherine Anne Porter

Writing letters may be the most commonly and widely used form of writing today. In general, people seem more relaxed when writing letters than writing in other forms such as poetry or fiction.

We all know how to write a letter. It's perhaps the form of writing that's taught in grade school earlier than anything else. We know the rhythm of it: the date, the greeting, the offering of formal pleasantries, the body of the letter, the well-wishing prior to the farewell, and the closing. The final "Sincerely yours," or "Love," is like a wave good-bye. We are comfortable with this form.

A familiar form like letters can be helpful because we don't have to learn the form in order to use it. It's easy to add this variety to our daily writing. What we will look at in this chapter are new ways to use this form in recovery and life.

Benefits of Writing to Someone

Letter writing provides us an audience that is often missing when we write in diaries. The question of who we are writing to in our journals disturbs some diarists. They may secretly believe that someone, perhaps a relative, will discover their journals stored in the attic. This can inhibit some writers and cause them to censor or embellish information.

Think of a friend you haven't spoken with for a few years. Possibly someone whom you won't likely see in the near future. Do you remember what that person drew out of you? Can you recall the unique energy and personality belonging to that relationship? Well, writing letters to that individual will draw out the same energy that you may not have expressed lately. When we lose a friend or travel away from someone, we often leave behind a part of ourselves that only lived in that relationship. Writing letters to that friend, even if we're not likely to see the person again, reawakens and brings that part of ourselves back.

If these people brought out a certain flair in us earlier, they can do the same for us in letters. This type of writing can be exciting and refreshing.

You needn't write so formally as addressing the person, "Dear. . ." or even dating the letter. These letters are not intended to be sent. You can begin by simply writing, "You."

Unsent Letters

Many letters we write, we write for ourselves, to clarify how we feel and think. Knowing we have no intention, at least initially, of sending the letters allows us to relax and write exactly what we feel, without fearing what the other person might think. If we decide, before writing, not to mail the letter, we may find ourselves more willing to write.

What happens when we write an unsent letter is that we focus on a particular "you" in the world, and this focus gives a new angle of vision and source for insight.

Perhaps you think we're talking about the angry letter. Angry letters have been spit out of many typewriters and recorded in many journals. This type of letter is commonly recommended to people in therapy to deal with resentment. This venting of anger through writing brings relief to a lot of people. But there are other kinds of unsent letters that are equally beneficial.

We can write a letter to a friend telling him or her that we value our friendship, something we've never said before. We can write letters to people we've lost touch with, as a way of reviewing our own lives. We can write letters to our children, even unborn children, as a way of extending our hopes into the world. If we have finished therapy, we can extend our learning by talking to the therapist through unsent letters.

In many cases, the letters may very well be mailed. Sheila R., a member of Adult Children Of Alcoholics, writes below about the indecision she felt about sending a letter to a friend. She had ended the letter with "I love you," and felt scared about it. It was lunchtime and she was at work, ready to drop the letter in the outgoing mail basket.

> I had decided to say "I love you." It seemed an important thing to do, precisely because it was extremely difficult. It needed to become easier. I decided that rather than wait for opportunities to arise, I would create them.
>
> Why, then, was I waffling?
>
> Fear. If I say "I love you," the person will go away.
>
> I come from what is termed a dysfunctional family. As a child, I learned that my feelings had a powerful effect. Adults were scared by them. Anger was forbidden; unfortunately, so was love.
>
> The longer the letter sat in that basket, the less urgent it seemed. I was losing faith in my intuition. The impulse now seemed an emotional outburst, a form of hysteria.

Take a deep breath. Remember the importance of ritual and practice. In putting the words "I love you" on paper, I made them real. I give myself permission to feel. I have to do that first, without guarantee of a positive response. Once written, the words become easier to say aloud. Not everyone is panicked by "love." I begin in safety with the friend I trust the most.

I need to do this for me.

I checked on the letter once or twice. Finally, the office runner picked it up and I could no longer retrieve it.

A few days later my friend called, "I love you, too."

Be thou my vision, not fear, not self-hatred, not the past. I seek my Higher Power through prayer, meditation, and song.

— Sheila R.

Of course, not all the letters you write will cause such a crisis. The decision to send or not to send your letters will be left up to you. We will discuss the letters as unsent in hope that this will encourage you to write more and be less inhibited.

In what follows, you will find suggestions on how to use letter writing more broadly in your recovery and life. We suggest writing letters:

- To Angels,
- To God or Your Higher Power,
- To Strangers,
- Letters of Gratitude or Appreciation,
- To Children, Parents, Spouses and Partners, and Siblings,
- To the Deceased,
- To Your Future.

Letters to an Angel

We first came across this idea in a book called, *The Dynamic Laws of Prosperity,* by Catherine Ponder. Ponder suggests we write to the angels of people who may be aggravating us in some way. These people could be a spouse during a divorce, an employer, a roommate, or even a clerk at the corner drugstore. Certainly, we don't like everyone. Writing a letter that appeals to that person's angel can be an intriguing creative effort. Many of us think it's unlikely that angels wearing long white gowns with massive wings even exist. We might, however, think that these people who aggravate us, for whatever reason, do in fact have a metaphorical angel, an "angelic" side to them, a good spirit somewhere inside them. We appeal, through a letter, to their good spirit, to that better or cooperative self in them. The angel can represent the individual's "higher self." For some of us, even this may be hard to believe because we think he or she is heartless. But try it. This exercise can produce surprising results.

After writing this letter, you may find yourself a bit more detached from the individual, less irked by the person. If you're lucky, you'll find that your next meeting with this person will go more smoothly.

Letters to God or Your Higher Power

Many of us saw the award-winning movie, *The Color Purple.* As we mentioned in an earlier chapter, Alice Walker's book from which the movie was made actually consists of letters to God. She uses the letters to tell God about things that happen to her and her family. Perhaps, there was no one else she could speak to. Another example of a writer addressing God can be found in the works of the reknowned German poet, Rainer Rilke. As a young man, he wrote a book called *Stories To God.* In a sense, his entire book was a letter addressed to this Power greater than himself.

We told you about one of our students who, instead of addressing her entries, "Dear Diary," wrote "Dear God." She says that she still begins her diary or journal in this way. Of course, she explains, "My idea of God has grown and matured." And this is precisely what writing letters to God might do for you. You may want to apply this exercise to your Eleventh Step work, hoping that a series of letters to your

Higher Power may increase your "conscious contact with God."

Finally, we suggest you try writing your own letter to God or your Higher Power.

Letters to Strangers

Have you ever read a newspaper article and found yourself deeply moved? Have you ever read a book and felt immensely grateful after finishing it? Have you ever seen a victim of a natural disaster on television, and for some reason you felt akin to the person? Has a friend ever described someone you immediately felt attracted to, though you never met the person? The individual in the newspaper article, the author of the book, the victim of the natural disaster, and the person your friend described are all strangers that emotionally touched you.

Think about addressing these people in letters. They will undoubtedly draw out something you need to express. An example of this comes from a woman who heard another woman on a tape in therapy. She discusses what she wrote.

> I first wrote a letter to a stranger when I was in therapy. It was a letter of appreciation. I had been doing a lot of work on the abuse I experienced in my childhood. My therapist played a tape, made by another woman struggling to heal, to be healed, and I sat and cried and cried. I was moved by her courage at being public. Now, years later, I can talk publicly about sexual abuse, but on that day I thought I would die if I ever had to tell anyone else but my therapist. My first step in overcoming shame was writing this letter to the woman on the tape. It wasn't a long letter, it was more of a note. For all I know now — it could have been written on flowered paper instead of in my journal. I can't even remember. But it was like lighting dynamite inside me. It was a big part of overcoming my isolation and shame. Life went on. I discovered that there were other people out there in the world I admired. If I felt like telling

them, I did. It was a wonderful feeling. Some of the letters I mailed, and some I didn't.

In this case, the woman's letter to a stranger helped her break through barriers of shame. Her letter was her coming out. She found a way to share her experience with someone other than her therapist. As most people in recovery know, it is critical to share your experiences with others; a letter enabled her to do this. In the same way, each of us can discover by writing to strangers something about ourselves that we might not have known.

A man in his forties would occasionally read a newspaper article and be especially moved by it. The post office tragedy in Edmonton, Oklahoma a few years ago when fourteen people were murdered was one of those events. This man felt shocked and saddened. There was no particular reason why this tragedy should have affected him more than any other, but it did. He accepted his feeling of connection. After putting down the newspaper, he went to his diary and addressed his entry to the entire town. He referred to the town of Edmonton as "you," collectively, as a single person. By doing this, the article was no longer "a typically tragic newspaper story." Later, he excerpted the entry from his diary and wrote it into a poem.

These two examples clearly show how strangers can deeply affect our lives. Writing letters to these strangers will help us to focus our lives.

Nobel prize winner, Saul Bellow, was ingenious in his use of this kind of writing. In his novel, *Herzog*, the protagonist, Moses Herzog "felt confident, cheerful, clairvoyant and strong. He had fallen under a spell and was writing letters to everyone under the sun." He wrote letter after letter, presumably unread, to famous people throughout the country. He wrote President Eisenhower, editors and publishers; he wrote to philosophers like Martin Heidegger; he even wrote to Tolstoy.

What "famous people," living or dead, would you chose to write? Imagine writing the humanitarian, civil rights leader, and Nobel Peace Prize winner Martin Luther King, or Nobel Peace Prize winner Mother Theresa. These people call up responses, feelings, and thoughts quite different from other people like Charlie Chaplin, Cary Grant, Marilyn Monroe, or even Jim Thorpe, the famous athlete. Select someone who creates a strong response in you and write that person a letter.

Letters of Gratitude

When we have lost someone to death, divorce, separation, or for other reasons, writing a letter of gratitude and appreciation sometimes may move us through the grief much faster than when we focus on the pain of loss.

It seems that in our culture many people are devastated by the loss of grandparents, even more so than parents. This is probably because we may be able to have such *pure* feelings of love for our grandparents. The death hits us in an acute, stabbing pain. Writer Jan Milner wrote the following piece for her grandmother, to get back some of her loving feelings and lessen her sense of loss. It's called "Letter To My Grandmother."

> When you tried to tell me what you'd leave for me someday, my eyes said no. . . . Now, when the phone rings at odd hours, I'm afraid it says, too late, too late. And I'm caught in the first line of the letter that begins, There are so many things I want to say before. . . I can't finish that first line. Make this an ordinary thank you note. A beginning: Dear Grandma, Thank you very much for sleep. On nights when I can't sleep I close my eyes and I remember whirling miles in the blue Dodge, and when we passed the city limits Iron Mountain dazzled like the Emerald City. I'm here for the whole summer. Then, keeping my eyes closed, I sniff the mint by the back door and go down in the

basement. The wringer washer here, the shrouded mangle huge in the corner. The walls cool on my fore-head. I lift the second back hall stair. Your black zip-up overshoes. The gum drawer in the kitchen is full, and the same block of wood props the dining room win-dow, by the table, set for our big meal at noon. You have covered Grandpa's grey, snoring chair. Curled up in it I hear the front porch awning slap the screen. Upstairs I touch the scratches the fireman made taking off the bathroom door when I couldn't work the lock. Even the air in your room is holy. I crouch in the attic sifting treasure, and climb down rubbing dust. I've saved my room for last. When I look in, there's a little girl in bed. She's closing a book and you are snapping off the light. You've just said, "Shall I hear your prayers?" And then I say that prayer you taught me and we say amen together. And I sleep.

— Jan Milner

Try writing a letter of appreciation to someone you know, living or dead. This letter could even be addressed to an ex-spouse, someone once loved but no longer loved in the same way. Use this exercise as a way of moving yourself through loss, grief, and toward letting go.

The next letter illustrates another example of letters of grati-tude. It was written to an author in appreciation of a pamphlet he had written on forgiveness. This letter could also be a good example of a letter to a stranger since the author did not know the sender. It's written by an AA member named Paul A.

I've just had one of those mountain top experiences that comes to us occasionally while we trudge the road of happy destiny and don't drink. I had picked up a group of materials that I hand out at a correctional facility. Somehow I bought one on "Forgiveness" though I don't know why, and brought that back home with me. It was the small pamphlet you wrote.

Well. . . .I decided to just give a try to the "active imagery" and talk to my divorced but still unforgiven wife. . . .I told her about what I resented, about the things she'd done. Then I asked her to forgive me for the things I'd done. I thought about her experiences with the two men in her life she really loved, her father and me, and how both of us hurt her deeply. . . .It wasn't easy to say . . . .I forgive you for all the things that have hurt me. . . .It was an amazing experience and to think all this happened as I sat talking to an empty chair with the image of my former wife there. It was as if she were right in the room.

I've still some more people I have to ask to sit in that magic chair. . . .Thank you for your help for me in your pamphlet; it hit me right between the eyes. It's going to become one of my cherished pieces of AA writings.
— Paul A.

Next time you come across a good book or pamphlet that you find especially moving, write the author a letter of gratitude. Besides pleasing the author, the letter may lift your spirits, too, into the sky of gratitude.

Letters to the Deceased

Many of us are troubled by leftover feelings that never got expressed to members of our families, friends, school chums, or even acquaintances who have died. We may regret that we never attended their funerals and failed to express our love to them. Years can go by before we even realize how deeply we miss these people. During active alcoholism, some alcoholics never attended the funerals of their parents. Drugs and alcohol may have numbed any real experience of grief. Now, in sobriety, people are able to face the absence of key, important people. Letter writing is one way we can use writing to communicate with the dead.

Before trying this exercise, spend some time thinking of someone you loved who has died. Try and recall specific events where the two of you were bonded. Were you twelve years old? Was it a sunny day in May and you sat with this person under an old, gnarled oak tree on the edge of a baseball diamond? Were you in the attic together on a Saturday afternoon rummaging through an old trunk, or outside learning how to change your bike's flat tire? You might start your letter to this deceased individual with simple details. Try to be as specific as possible. Too much abstraction may sanitize the experience. If your letter goes on and on about "how much I miss you, I wish you were here, you were my best friend, I love you, I grieve..." the problem becomes indistinct. Be specific. Remember how important this is. Specifics will eventually lead you to a greater intensity in your writing, as well as feeling.

After you've written a letter to someone deceased, the question of what to do with the letter arises. Of course, you don't have to do anything with it. You can tear it up, share it with someone else who knew the individual, or simply save it to review in the future. We've heard of people who mail them to fictitious addresses, with no return address. In this way, they send the letter out to the world and let go of it. Letters can be mailed to the families of the deceased. You can take the letters to the grave site and read them aloud, burn them at home, or, having found yourself satisfied and moved by what you discovered in your writing, you might just file the letter away. Any one of the rituals mentioned above might give you a sense of resolution.

Letters to Family Members

In the following sections, we're going to ask you to consider writing letters to different family members. If you have a child, you might consider writing the child a letter, focusing on his or her first day at nursery school, an amusing anecdote that reveals a startling insight, or your child's first date. If you're married or have a significant other, think about writing that person a letter. You could address certain memories you have of your grandparents. First, we will concern ourselves with writing letters to children.

Letters to Children

One father wrote the following entry in his diary:

Dear Daughter,

It was really neat to see you dancing at summer school yesterday. I know you take it for granted that you are a good dancer, but I want you to know that I enjoyed the dancing. You've been saying for three years now that you wanted to find something you were really good at. Hooray, you found tennis this summer. Other people thought you were good at dancing but what's important is for you to love something of your own. I know you're glad when you say, "I finally found something I'm good at — tennis."

Love, Dad

This is a simple letter, like a note; any one of us could have written it. Whether you decide to actually show it or read it to your child is your decision. Sometimes, sharing our entries can be especially heartwarming. The point is that addressing a particular person in your family through a letter requires us to write in a language that is simpler and more direct. The father's letter is an appreciative letter, and it's as important to express our gratitude as well as our anger.

If you have children, you might write several letters to them. Later, read the letters over and select one or parts from each of them and rewrite them. Then seal the letter in an envelope and store it somewhere for when the child gets older. You can make this exercise a part of your New Year resolution to write a letter to your child each year. (If you have no children of your own, consider writing to a favorite nephew or niece.)

Don't fool yourself into trying to write "profound" things.

Our writing is most profound and moving when we are not trying to be. Keep it simple. Describe how the child looks to you at that age. Describe his rosy cheeks on a winter day when he came in through the backdoor after shoveling snow with his red plastic shovel. Write about his long legs, thick hair, the wisp of a curl. Mention a particular night that might reflect the trouble you may have had getting the child to bed. Write those things you wish your parents wrote about you. Wouldn't you be happy now to receive twenty letters, a letter for each of your first twenty years that your parents wrote and saved for you? So would your child. Begin today by writing the first letter.

Letters can be written to an unborn child. One mother we know wrote daily during her pregnancy and later excerpted the entries to use for a magazine article. Letters to the unborn could involve writing to an imaginary child who was aborted or miscarried. Parents who decide to give their children up for adoption might use this writing technique.

Letters to Parents

You may be surprised by what you write. You may sit back and think, *I never realized how happy I was to hear my dad's car pull up the driveway every evening. Or I'll never forget my mother brushing my hair, smelling her perfume.* Letters that reawaken joyful memories like these are especially precious.

Letters to our mothers and fathers can be very significant in recovery. The German novelist, Franz Kafka, known for his surrealistic and bizarre stories, wrote a very touching book called *Letter To His Father.* This book or letter was originally intended to be sent, but never was. Kafka begins his letter exploring why he felt afraid of his father. He attempts to understand the breach between father and son, hoping to restore a relationship that had been emotionally bruised. Reading this book, one can't help but feel how powerfully moved Kafka was in the actual writing. In the same way, letters to our parents can lead us to new insights. Again, the focus of this exercise should be on ourselves. We are not out to get even with our parents; we are writing for ourselves, not for them.

It is sad to think that Kafka died without ever feeling the breach was healed; yet writing validated the fact that the breach existed and that his fear was real. Unsent letters to parents can also assist us in our grief process and help us let go of resentments. Some people from dysfunctional families may need the support of a therapist to write letters to their parents.

Letters to Spouses and Partners

Another idea for a letter is one to your spouse or partner. For example, we've included the letter below written as a poem by poet Robert Hass to his wife while he was apart from her. He titled the poem, "Letter."

> I had wanted to begin
> by telling you I saw another
> tanager below the pond
> where I had sat for half an hour
> feeding on wild berries
> in the little clearing near the pines
> that hide the lower field
> and then looked up from red berries
> to the quick red bird brilliant
> in the light. I have seen
> more yarrow and swaying
> Queen Anne's lace around the woods
> as hawkweed and nightshade
> wither and drop seed. A new blue flower,
> sweet, yellow-stamened, ovary inferior,
> has recently sprung up.
>   But I had the odd
> feeling, walking to the house
> to write this down, that I had left
> the birds and flowers in the field,
> rooted or feeding. They are not in my

head, are not now on this page.
It was very strange to me, but I think
their loss was your absence. I wanted
to be walking up with Leif, the sun
behind us skipping off the pond,
the windy maple sheltering the house,
and find you there and say
here! a new blue flower (ovary inferior)
and busy Leif and Kris with naming
in a world I love. You even have
my field guide. It's you I love.
I have believed so long
in the magic of names and poems.
I hadn't thought them bodiless
at all. Tall Buttercup. Wild Vetch.
"Often I am permitted to return
to a meadow." It all seemed real to me
last week. Words. You are the body
of my world, root and flower, the
brightness and surprise of birds.
I miss you, love. Tell Leif
you're the name of things.

— Robert Hass

Letters to Siblings

Finally, writing letters can affirm our closeness to siblings. The letter may even make amends and heal old wounds. The poem, "Moving Away," by Gary Soto, is written like a letter to his brother.

Remember that we are moving away   brother
From those years
In the same house with a white stepfather
What troubled him has been forgotten
But what troubled us has settled

like dirt
In the nests of our knuckles
And cannot be washed away

All those times you woke shivering
In the night
From a coldness I
Could not understand
And cupped a crucifix beneath the covers

All those summers we hoed our yard
In the afternoon sun
The heat waving across our faces
And we waved back wasps
While the one we hated
Watched from under a tree and said nothing

We will remember those moments   brother
And now that we are far
From one another
What I want to speak of
Is the quiet of a room just before daybreak
And you next to me   sleeping

— Gary Soto

The poem brings to the surface bitter memories the two brothers have of their "white stepfather." Yet, at the end, the poem creates a nurturing image of a quiet room where the brothers are in bed "just before daybreak." The poem seems to be saying that for Soto the tenderness he has for his brother remains stronger than the memories of pain.

Now, try addressing a letter to someone in your family. Choose anyone of the examples for inspiration. What you write can be a simple expression of love, as in the first example by a father to his daughter, or it can express complicated relationships as in Soto's poem. Whatever you chose to do, let the writing come out of your heart, as straightforward as possible. Be honest and direct. In the past, you may not have even considered this a writing exercise. Some people hold onto resentments for a long time and these resentments contributed to the dysfunctioning of the family. Now, they can participate in the healing of the family.

Letters to a Future

Living one day at a time requires tremendous focus, energy, and discipline. To keep our minds and hearts focused on what is in front of us demands our attention. Yet, many of us find ourselves waking early in the morning, ruminating on a past or future event. There's nothing wrong with this unless our thinking becomes obsessive and begins interfering with our enjoyment of the moment. Then, writing a letter to the past or future might help us gather energy more purposefully and direct it more usefully. Here is an example of one.

Dear Future,

Today I am walking down Portland Ave. thinking about you, trying to guess what you'd prefer me to wear next week when I attend my brother's wedding. Should I wear my blue suit or gray one? I worry about you. What plans you have for me. Sometimes, I imagine you sitting in a rocking chair, on a porch reading my manuscript and frowning. You decide it's terrible, tear the pages one by one. When I come, you have the police handcuff me, make me promise to never try to write poetry again, and have me swear to find an eight-to-five job.

Write a letter expressing your hopes for the week. Write down the things you hope to accomplish for that week. Include feelings you want to have. Of course, the week will inevitably surprise you with something you haven't imagined. Try then, in your letter, to imagine what surprises the week has in store for you. If you have an important appointment that week, include in your letter what you hope will happen. Set a reasonable goal that you intend to achieve and include this in the letter. At the end of the week, open the letter and enjoy it. You could apply this to the your Tenth Step work, using the letter to take an inventory of the week.

Writing Letters and the Ninth Step

Earlier, we mentioned how you might apply letter writing to your Ninth Step work. We thought a more detailed section might be helpful, since letter writing can be effective in making amends.

Often making amends does not involve writing letters. Sometimes letting go of a grudge is all that is needed. At other times, a change in behavior is a way to make amends, and no language is necessary. At still other times, meeting with the person and talking directly is necessary.

Sometimes, however, a written apology is called for. Letters are a wonderful communication tool for complicated issues because they allow both sides time to reflect and cool off before answering. When you write a letter to make amends, you can give yourself the freedom to write it first and then hold it until you are ready to mail it.

Sometimes it is terrifying to apologize, because you have absolutely no control over the other person's reaction, or how that person will use the information in the letter. It's good to remember that the reason you're writing is to change your behavior from being resentful to being forgiving. Making this change in behavior is the best amends you can make.

Sending the words out into the world can help you get healthier, no matter what the other person does with the letter. Your most felicitous apology may be met with anger, or worse, silence. But once you have admitted what you did, you will be able to move on, regardless of the outcome.

Writing a letter to make amends can prepare you, that is, help you to rehearse a face-to-face meeting, even if you never mail it. Think about someone who you still need to make amends to. If you've already decided that amends need to be made in person, then first try writing the amends in a letter. Again, describe exactly what behavior you want to apologize for. You might even describe the place where you might meet this person and create a more real atmosphere.

CHAPTER 8

"Whither Thou Goest, I Will Go": Telling Our Stories

> There are only two or three human stories and they go on repeating themselves as fiercely as if they had never happened before.
> —Willa Cather

People have been telling stories since the beginning of our time on earth. We tell stories about the stars, about how the world came into existence, about how a cow kicking a bucket started the Great Chicago Fire. Gossip and rumor and news exist in every country, at every gathering, in every group. Long before we had written language, we had stories, and they were passed along from one generation to the next by memorizing and telling and repeating. This process is called *oral tradition*, and it exists today among families and groups.

What does story telling give to us? A story gives us one view of the world. A story reveals the world. A story says, "This is the way life is." When we hear people tell how they recovered from incredible adversity, our awareness of the world is enlarged. In this way, stories represent connection to other people, and to a spiritual power larger than ourselves.

When we tell a story, we give ourselves a way to express our identity. We give a shape and wholeness to our lives by the stories that we tell.

Although stories represent one view of reality, they are also, in some mysterious manner, open-ended. The story itself is stronger than the message that the teller may add to it. As listeners, we take from a story our own idea of what's important in it. In this way, stories offer freedom to the listeners. "Take what you can use and leave the rest," a common theme in Twelve Step programs, also applies to stories.

As an example of the core meaning of a story, and the listener's freedom to interpret it, consider the story of Ruth and Naomi, one of the oldest stories in the Judeo-Christian tradition. This story is at least twenty-five hundred years old; it may have existed longer in the oral tradition. How did this story last so long? Partly because it was written down, but also because the story contains elements that are compelling, elements that are worth being remembered, and worth being retold. But what is the story? Do you remember it?

We didn't remember it exactly. We thought that Ruth and Naomi had a close and loving relationship that was stronger than any law or legal bond. When Ruth's husband died, she decided to stay with her mother-in-law, Naomi, rather than return to her own homeland. She said the words that we've used as this chapter's title, "Whither thou goest, I will go..." We couldn't remember any more of the story, but we were touched by the power of these words, the calmness and passion inherent in them.

We started asking people what they remembered about Ruth and Naomi. Most people could only remember a small part of the story, yet each person held a nugget of meaning, a sense of the crucial core of the story. Here are some of the random comments people made. You'll notice that they vary widely.

> Oh, yeah, Ruth and Naomi. I was always impressed that they decided to travel together. It was dangerous for women to travel without men in those days. They were brave.

We always heard the story at our church's mother-daughter banquet and I always felt inadequate because I didn't think I'd ever love anyone that much. I thought I could never live up to it.

Ruth and Naomi — it's a story about great love and devotion.

They went to pick up grain in the fields, they were gleaners, that's what they did for welfare in those days, and then Naomi told Ruth to go sleep at Boaz's feet and maybe he'd notice her. Well, I'd think you'd notice someone sleeping in your room.

Isn't that the story that Shubert made a song out of that they always sing at weddings? I am moved when I hear the song because it's saying that the friendship between two women is the model for how a marriage should be.

When we looked the story up and reread it, we discovered that Ruth and Naomi did make a pact for life that they both kept. They traveled to a new country and made a new life together. Each comment listed above is accurate. Each one reveals a slightly different angle on the story.

So we can see from this story that stories come and go, and that the core of a story can change over time and with each listener.

What we'll work on in this chapter is writing some of the stories that we already have within us. We will put our energy to work writing the stories we already know, and tell stories about our own lives.

The sections of this chapter are:

- Writing Down a Story from Your Oral Tradition
- Writing a History from Your Life
- Stories in Twelve Step Programs
- Changing Stories: Coming Out With Our Truer Selves
- Moving from Story to Fiction

Writing Down a Story from Your Oral Tradition

Think back to all the stories that you've heard told in your family as part of your family's oral tradition. You may love your family or you may hate your family; either way, all the family stories are inside of you, unexamined, until you let them out by telling them or writing them down. When they are out of you and down on paper, you can decide if you want to keep them.

Here is one way to begin: Make a list of the stories you remember hearing as you were growing up, stories you heard more than once. Here's a sample.

- Why Van Gogh Cut Off His Ear
- Betty's Pony
- Why Grandpa Charlie Made the Children Hold Books Under Their Elbows
- When We Lived on the Farm and the Bums Came Knocking
- Mama's Grave
- Drying Apples by Putting Them on the Roof
- The Gold Chain
- Why Nobody Wants to Go to Kansas City to Visit Our Kin
- The Night Dad Threw the Dishrag at Mom
- Eleanor Roosevelt

See how many stories you can list. Then pick the story that seems to call out to you today. Remember, a story is open-ended. You don't have to know what it means or why you feel drawn to it. Now, start writing the story as completely as you remember it. Write as though you are talking, telling the story to someone else. Write the story just the way you heard it grow-ing up, with this one exception: include at least one conversa-tion. In literary terms, a conversation is called dialogue. And dialogue brings a story to life. Remember that some people recall nothing but the dialogue between Ruth and Naomi, "Whither thou goest..."

Some family stories are quickly told. You may be done by

the end of one sheet of paper. Other stories go on and on. Don't worry about whether the story is long or short. The point is to see that stories you've heard all your life can be a source of writing for you. When you're done, congratulate yourself for bringing a story out of the oral tradition onto paper.

Writing down family stories is a good warm-up for story writing. At the end of this chapter, we'll look at one way of extending a family story into a longer piece of writing, a short story. For now, though, you might want to write several family stories and see which ones come out the most easily.

Writing a History from Your Life

Everyone has many histories, many stories. We each have a work history, a sexual history, a school history, a medical history. Each one of these histories reflects a separate aspect of our lives. They may go by different names: our medical history may be called up by the words *charts and records*. Our school history may be reflected by the words *transcripts*.

But whatever words we call them, each history shows one aspect of our lives, which weaves together with our other histories to make one story. We could call these histories *strands* or *threads*, to get the sense of many stories weaving together.

When we write about our lives, we can quickly become overwhelmed by the wealth of information and contradictions. But if we write about one strand, we can ignore everything else and concentrate on this one reality. This focus simplifies the writing process.

The other advantage of writing one history is that it helps us take the long view of our lives; it helps us see the many changes we've been through. We can see crisis, resolutions, and progress. We can see how we've changed over time.

Here are some suggested titles for a history:

- The History of My Writing
- The Story of Me and Booze

- My Love Affair with Automobiles
- Me and Money
- Sexuality, Sexual Preference, Yes, No, I Forgot
- My Love-Hate Relationship with School
- Work, Work, Work
- History of My Spirituality
- Fly Fishing and Me

We'd like you to pick one of these titles or choose one of your own. The directions for this are very simple because, as we said, picking the topic for a history limits what's going to happen. The structure for the writing is already there.

Once you've picked the topic, take the long view of your life. Try to cover the significant aspects of this topic. Think about the milestones. You could think of moments of significant insight. You could think of turning points. Keep an eye out for changes in attitudes, and changes in behaviors. You may include dialogue and description, but don't spend too much time on dialogue and description because it will slow you down. You're supposed to cover your whole life in a couple of pages. Let your history emerge in all its fullness and contradiction.

You may try writing on automatic pilot and see how fast you can zip through your life. Here is an example of a first draft of stream-of-consciousness work on "History of My Writing." Notice how the writer skips along over many years, in fragmented sentences.

> The crayons, those big boxes that cost a buck that my mother shelled out unwillingly. The square and yellow and green crayola box with the crayon sharpener at one end, on the side, on the bottom. The crayolas that melted under the window of the green bullet-nosed Studebaker leaving the waxy permanence on the gray fabric of the...whatever-the-hell-you-call-it...little deck/dust catcher under the window. The first grade teacher made the belly of the A go left and the stem

came down. The vowels were my friends, consonants were like the snotty kid who lived across the street, Roy. . .Third grade I used an ink pen on an assignment instead of a pencil — Sister Leona slapped my face, said I had my nerve & she thought I was such a good student like my father had been — we weren't supposed to be using pens until after Christmas & then we'd start using them together — the right way.

— Jimmy Olson

When we read this history, we may wonder, *Who was this Sister Leona? Did she turn off this person from writing forever?* We will have to wait until the writer finishes the history to know how significant these moments were in his overall life. Maybe this memory was a surprise to the writer.

Writing a history seems to bring forth surprises for most people. Writing a history also seems to bring up questions and reflections about what is unfolding. It's okay to write in your reactions as you go, to write in thoughts and questions, speculations. But keep moving. Keep your pencil moving across the page. Don't stop for more than a paragraph with your own commentary on the flow of time. For example, an AA member who was writing her history of work and money stopped to ask herself these questions.

Was I really responsible for not having saved any money by age 36? Wasn't it my parents' fault because they had never taught me about money? Had I decided to spend my salary on fast sports cars, an expensive piano I rarely played, grandiose presents for lovers — beautiful things — with no thought to my future?

— Susan C.

Questions can be valuable for you later, as you decide which times of your life are the milestones you want to keep in your history. But don't let the questions slow you down. Keep moving. Don't get stuck in any one time period. You can go back later.

Here's an example of a history written by a Twelve Step program member. It could be titled *History of My Spirituality*, but it's not; it's titled, *Higher Power, Awakening, and Sensible Clothes*. Writing this history surprised the writer in a way we'll discuss after you've read it.

> I remember being awakened in second grade when I read Anderson's *The Snow Queen* and was captured forever by the little robber girl. When the heroine was stripped of her golden carriage (lined with sugar plums), it was the robber girl who protected her, questioned the hard journey, spoke frankly of danger, and dressed her in sensible clothes. This little thug also provided Gerda, the heroine, with a reindeer who knew the way to the Snow Queen's palace. In a world of stories about "nice" girls and magic endings and things as useless as golden coaches lined with sugar plums, the little robber girl was a blazing comet of truth. I trusted her.
>
> I didn't trust the saints and martyrs that I read about in my Catholic classrooms nor did I trust the stories about the "good" children included in our readers. A third grade story I still recall with anger involved a child named Mary who went out in a snowstorm to help her ailing mother. Mary wore a thin dress and sandals to complete this mission of mercy. Her mother recovered and Mary died. I was disgusted and thought at the time that she should have run into the little robber girl. But who needed thieves when one had the company of angels? I decided I did, if I were to survive my good intentions. I enlisted in the company of outlaws — quietly.
>
> Still, I went to church often and prayed to be let in on the great secret. What was it about the women who

were spiritually advanced and respected that I didn't understand? The churches were stone cold and the statues were rooted in their robes, staring, frozen. Clothing seemed to pour from heaven itself, covering heads, bodies, legs and feet. Everything about them was cast in stone. No heart beat, no stomach growled. I imagined being cast in such clothing until my body disappeared altogether and there was nothing left of me but a gentle, resigned smile of acceptance. At such times I felt I had caught on, and I would leave the church feeling what I thought was deep peace. Within hours, rage would erupt. I never knew why or where it came from. I felt "bad" and lonely for angels.

During the summer of fourth grade, I went to the capitol grounds of Bismarck, North Dakota, and stood beneath the statue of Sacajawea. I felt awake again. Energy poured from her to me. I looked at her amazed: she had LEGS! Her feet touched the ground. She wore clothes suitable for a long journey. She was a woman in motion and her eyes, fixed on a distant goal, were confident and interested. She communicated LIFE to me. The more I looked at her, the stronger I felt, and as I looked, stories bloomed in me — about journeys, knowledge, pathfinding, cleverness, about not belonging but knowing how to get from here to there. When I left her I took the stories and the feeling of strength and the image of layers of clothes, rippled with journey and motion, suiting the wearer and the path she was on.

Years later, after the uniforms and the formals, the wedding dress and maternity clothes, I stepped into unknown territory. Behind me was a shattered marriage, angers and regrets, the death of many dreams. I was stripped of the golden carriage, the sugar plums, and the chemicals that kept me dependent. I didn't know the path I was on and most certainly did not know the way. As I searched for a guide, sifting through spiritual readings and biographies, what kept surfacing was the feeling that I already was very familiar with my guides. "Well, show yourselves!" I challenged, bracing for bright lights and whirring wings.

Softly, softly, like a forest elf, the little robber girl crept back and as I looked up I saw the confident stride of Sacajawea walking across the night sky. I am so grateful to have them back. I can trust them. They know the way and they will not let me go off on my journey without sensible clothes.

— Ann

When you read this wonderful history, you might notice that Ann covers her whole life in two pages, yet she doesn't tell us the *whole story* of her life; she tells us the high points of one aspect of her life. Remember what we said about surprises? Ann says that when she started working on this history, she had no awareness of sensible clothes being part of this spiritual history until she was in the middle of writing. The title she selected for this history honors the surprises our spirit gives us.

Now you do one.

Stories in Twelve Step Programs

Telling stories is a central part of Twelve Step programs. People learn how the program works by listening to the stories of other people. The most succinct statement is perhaps an early sentence in the book *Alcoholics Anonymous*, from the chapter titled "How It Works."

Our stories disclose in a general way what we used to be like, what happened, and what we are like now.

When people talk in a meeting, they tell stories.

- They may tell a story that illustrates a lesson.
- They may tell their own story of recovery.

In this section, we're going to look at these two kinds of stories.

Writing Stories that Illustrate a Lesson

All the great teachers — spiritual teachers, school teachers, political leaders — use stories as a tool. Sometimes stories are called *illustrations*, or *fables*. There's something about a story that stays with us longer than abstract statements because a story is a series of connected actions, and the actions give us pictures in our minds. When we are babies, we learn about the world through touch, sight, and sound. We learn the meanings of words slowly as we grow. Abstract thought is something we learn *after* infancy. Pictures and sounds connect with our early life in a powerful way that abstract sentences can never do. Creating pictures with words is important in stories, just as it is in poems.

For example, if I ask you to donate money to a halfway house for runaways, you may hesitate. But if I tell you that a halfway house may have to shut down if it doesn't get more funding, and one of the clients is John, a fourteen-year-old boy who used to work as a prostitute because he had no place else to go, you may still hesitate, but my appeal for money will have a story with it that you will remember longer than the abstract question, "Can you give to a halfway house?"

People tell stories because we remember stories. In any kind of situation, from a spiritual gathering to a fund drive, stories last longer in our minds than abstract statements. At Twelve Step meetings, people use stories to illustrate any and all of the changes that have happened in their lives. These stories range from something the person observed, to an anecdote from a personal history, to the description of a change in behavior.

The writer in the following example never used to notice what was going on around her. Now that she is more conscious, she is observant of the world. Rather than writing, "I see more now," she describes the scene outside her window, which she observes, now, every morning. It's the same window she used to stare out of and see nothing.

The pines outside are filled with bird chat. The crows have the most to say, are the loudest, bully the others. Sparrows are relentless. After giving up on seeing a grosbeak or a jay or a junco, I watch the sparrows and am surprised to find them interesting: colors, patterns of markings, even their dear ordinary faces hold light I've not noticed before. Early and late, but not the times between, I can expect cardinals: My Lady and Bright Guy. They, more than any, have trained me to be a responsible bird mom. She will sit patiently on a branch not far from my window where I write, cocking her head, ruffling feathers, shifting her balance. She gets my attention within minutes — recently, I've begun to anticipate her and can tell if she's just saying "hello" or "fill the feeder!" Perhaps some bird shaman has taught her to go to the three pines, move her head a certain number of times and she will be rewarded with food. She teaches me my limitations as a "god," and the sparrows astonish me with their plain beauty: all the ordinary miracles.

— Ann

This story represents for the writer one way her life has changed. The story *illustrates* a change.

It is important to talk for a moment how this kind of a story works in a meeting before we talk about writing a story like this one.

The way stories weave through a Twelve Step meeting often resembles what we might imagine as village life before writing and books, when exchanging stories was part of the fabric of the shared experience. Stories and anecdotes are the heart of the talk at a meeting. Dr. Thomas Lavin, a Jungian speaker, has said, "AA is the village for people who don't belong in the village."

People at the meeting respond to the speaker by telling their stories and anecdotes that resonate with the speaker's. The accumulation of stories is a mosaic of life experience. This is a very gentle call-and-response way of story telling. It weaves a group together.

In this kind of story telling, each person reflects on his or her own experience. There is no sermon, not even from the speaker, outlining the one right way. The speaker is nonjudgmental. The story is not telling other people how to act; rather, the speaker is saying, "This is how it was for me."

Writing a story that illustrates a lesson is perhaps the easiest writing exercise in this book. It's so easy, in fact, it may look hard. To get started, you might start out by saying, "Why, just the other day I realized..." Then, you might continue with your thoughts and a story, writing as if you were talking at a meeting.

If this does not come easily, here are some further directions. Think about your life recently. What are some changes that have come about in your life? What are some things you've noticed recently? Remember, you're looking for an event that gave you an insight, an illustration, a lesson. Here are some possible topics.

- Something you noticed in nature
- Something you noticed on the freeway
- A moment of being alone and not being lonely
- A change for the better in an old friendship
- A new friendship
- A moment when it seemed like you actually do have a manageable life
- Something you saw out in the world, on the streets

Pick a moment of insight and start writing. You might state the insight first, to help focus your writing. Then describe the scene that gave you the insight. It might be a description. It might be a conversation. It might be a straight story with lots of action, let's say a story about a car accident. It might include thoughts. After you're done, you may want to drop the original sentence that states the insight.

Telling Your Recovery Story

"Telling my story" is the phrase in Twelve Step programs that refers to telling one's life story of addiction and recovery. It weaves together anecdotes and histories into one life story. In telling the story, the speaker covers a whole life in a short amount of time.

The whole idea behind a "story" is that it will condense and unify, because it has a beginning, middle, and end. It progresses in an orderly fashion and ties everything together.

When you tell your story, you make a cohesive whole out of a life that may have been chaotic. The story gives a wholeness *simply in the telling.* When you are done telling your story, that life is now past tense, and the sense of ending frees you to move on. Telling your story also frees you from the judgmental part of the mind, because the story is "out there" in the very telling of it.

The process of telling the story of your life can be helpful to you even if you are not in a Twelve Step program. You might write the story of recovery from a divorce. You might write about your experiences recovering from a physical illness or an emotional condition. You might write about experiences with the military and war. You could write the story of your struggle with any kind of adversity and use the directions here to give a sense of wholeness to your struggle.

The process is healing to the teller and listener alike. As we mentioned in the previous section, telling stories, both life stories of recovery and stories that illustrate a lesson, is central to Twelve Step programs. The Big Book, *Alcoholics Anonymous,* is composed of many stories. It has nearly six hundred pages. Of these, nearly four hundred pages of the book are stories. There are forty-four personal stories, each one unique. The opening chapter of the book, "Bill's Story," is also a story. The fact that so many stories are in this text emphasizes both community and individualism; each story is unique, but each story has points of connection with other people's stories.

While the Big Book continues to be the touchstone book for recovering alcoholics, and books are modeled after it as touchstone books in other Twelve Step programs, other books with stories are also useful. For example, the book *The Courage to Change*, was put together by the talk show moderator Dennis Wholey. In this book are recovery stories of well-known people. It is an inspiring book. It is useful, for instance, to know what happened to Grace Slick after her years of singing "...feed your head." It is useful to know that not all rock stars die of an overdose. These stories work like the stories in meetings to give a clue about how recovery happens. Another useful book, *A Woman Like You*, edited by Rachel V., is a collection of stories of recovering women — middle-class women, poor women, Jewish women, women of color, lesbians and heterosexual women, women of all ages. The stories are instructive in the ways that women deal with the male image of God in the Twelve Steps. This book is a good companion volume to The Big Book because it balances the many stories of men in The Big Book. But what Rachel V. has to say in her introduction applies to both women and men.

> Storytelling of the kind that goes on in AA meetings is like a subversive activity. It restores value to a life that has been denied and suppressed; exiled dreams are reclaimed....Community is created between teller and listeners and love is restored.
>
> — Rachel V.

Another useful book for people who are doing family of origin work is a collection of fiction titled, *Family: Stories from the Interior*, edited by Geri Chavis.

Telling your story is a healing act. Writing it down adds a deeper dimension. Writing holds your story in time so that you can come back to it. A few years later, you can look back at it and see changes that have happened as your recovery continues. In this way, a written story represents a base for you to grow from. Writing your story also makes it available to sharing with more people. It exists as a completed version of your life.

Your story can be part of the work for Step One, Step Four, and Step Nine. Certainly, telling your story is one of the ways to move beyond the guilt of the past. Telling your story is a way to experience the promises mentioned in The Big Book: "We will not regret the past nor wish to shut the door on it."

Writing your story is a slow process. Let yourself relax until you can hear your own voice talking in your mind. Write down your voice talking the way you talk out loud. Then imagine the beginning, middle, and end of your story. Once you have the sense of where the beginning is, you are ready to start writing. You might start with your family background. Make this part a summary, no more than a paragraph. For example, Leah G. tells her story in *A Woman Like You*.

> I'm 50 years old and have been sober for sixteen years. I came from an average middle-class upbringing. My family was stable....I was not abused. I was never denied or deprived in any conceivable way. And still, I'm an alcoholic. It's a disease. Everyday folks, even Jewish women like me, suffer from it.
>
> — Leah G.

You might write next about your first high, the golden glow. Then detail certain scenes from your life that reveal a growing dependency. All the while, keep on moving so that you can cover your life in a short space. Leah G., again, summarizes many years with these words.

> Like many women, I was a very functional drunk.... My beds were made, my house was clean, my children were fed and tended. I didn't black out or get drunk in the ways that people could see. I functioned in my art, I was a good wife and mother....I denied and hid my alcoholism in the fact that I functioned. I did my drinking alone at night.
>
> — Leah G.

After showing — remember, *show, don't tell* — the progression of the addiction, move on to the time when you knew you were in trouble but didn't do anything about it. This is the stage of going from bad to worse. Try to find one day that exemplifies your denial. Try to find another time when your using caused you to engage in behaviors that violated your values. You don't need to tell everything.

At this point, you might include a conversation with a friend or partner who was trying to get you to see the light and get help. You might talk about how your addiction affected your work life, your home life, your friendships.

Next, you might describe in detail the circumstances of your living situation when you hit bottom. What happened that caused you to seek help? A friend? A loss? A court order? An intervention? Divine intervention? Describe the scene in detail. Leah G. describes her moment of realization in this way.

> I was totally lost. My life lost its focus. I rented a studio one day, and stood there in front of the mirror alone under the neon lights. I was thirty-four. I began to weep. I saw myself in the mirror, and I was an old woman. My skeleton peered through the flesh. I didn't stop drinking at this point, but I went back into therapy and started to get honest about my drinking. I don't think the man knew much about alcoholism, but he did his homework. One day out of the blue, he came in and said, "Leah, would you consider going to Alcoholics Anonymous?" I just remember sitting there in total silence. . . . I felt as if I had exhaled for the first time in thirty-four years.
>
> — Leah G.

After you've described your turning point — it may be the first of many, or the only one — go on and tell about your recovery process in a few paragraphs.

Now relate some events that have happened during your recovery. They may not all be wonderful. In fact, many peoples' most intensive losses come after they have gotten into recovery. Mention your struggles. All the while you are writing, keep in mind that you want to paint a rich picture of one person's recovery — your life in living color. It's like a television documentary that is edited down to one hour. You can't tell it all; so tell the "good parts."

Changing Stories: Coming Out with Our Truer Selves

Which stories are you drawn to? Which family stories do you tell and retell? Do you see your story changing? Certain stories hook us at different times in our lives. Think about your favorite books. What was your favorite in grade school? Recently, we asked a class of adults to think about their favorite books at age eighteen. Some people were somewhat embarrassed to admit their adolescent taste in books, for they no longer were attached to those books. Others were still in love with the writers of their youth. The list included *The Fountainhead*, *Another Country*, *Catcher in the Rye*, *On the Road*. The stories we are hooked on show us where we are, our sense of our place in the world. When we pay attention to the stories that we are drawn to, we can learn about where we are, and decide if we like this place or want to move on.

Any of the books that are loved by eighteen year olds could be limited if taken as a description of adult reality. We know that *On the Road* is a breath of fresh air for anyone growing up in a bourgeois home; yet it does not give a world view about what to do with life when one turns thirty. The author of *In My Father's House*, Sylvia Fraser, said in a recent television interview that she discovered that she had been an incest victim only after she'd published five novels and noticed at that point that her books contained much sexual violence. She paid attention to her stories and learned about her life. After she became aware, she wrote *In My Father's House*, the story of her childhood.

When we pay attention to the stories that we are drawn to, including our own stories, books we love, and family stories that have been passed down to us, we can use these stories as a guide to a healthier reality.

Stephen Peters, a fiction writer, has written an essay about family stories and their powerful hold over us. He talks about his process of trying to change his family's glorification of the military. Stephen and his brother argued bitterly about the Vietnam War. The brother served in Vietnam, survived, but died after the war from cancer. Stephen has tried to free his own son from the family message that if you want to be "a real man," you have to join the military. In his essay, Stephen described going to see the movie *Platoon* with Chris, his son, in a small mill town in Pennsylvania. He wanted to take his son to see *Platoon* because he thought it was a good anti-war movie. He wrote:

> My son knows that my brother and I disagreed about the war, that we fought bitterly, and that I still believe our father's bemedaled Army Air Corps uniform hanging in the attic all those years filled my brother's head with false notions and eventually got him killed for nothing.
>
> We lined up at the ticket window on the sidewalk and I remembered that on a quiet afternoon in summer, walking across the wide courthouse square and sucking up the stench of sulphur from the paper mill, you can hear them working the open pit mine a mile out of this town. This is home. The paper mill. The open pit mine. There are also steel mills and power plants nearby. It's deer hunter country. I trust what I see here. The people who work the mines and the mills are just the sort who get to fight wars, and they generally do not believe they can change or affect anything outside their families. They may raise hell with a six pack and a pick-up, but they do as they are told in the larger sense.

We got to the theater early and a handful of middle-aged men and women came in first and sat down to wait. Then the place filled up. High school kids on dates came in, dressed to kill and chewing gum. A group of teenaged boys in fatigue pants and pea green T-shirts trooped to the front and took up almost a whole row. I thought the smell of popcorn was heavier than it should have been. Except for those few men and women, the other early comers who sat silently, I thought the crowd too jittery, too wound up, too much like people filling seats on a roller coaster. The music played. People talked as Charlie Sheen and his buddies arrived in Vietnam, and as the Biblical injunction "Rejoice, O Young man, in your youth" appeared on the screen.

Then they cheered the explosion of Claymores at night — the rocket's red glare, you know. They clapped as Charlie Sheen took his first toke in the doper's bunker. And that final, terrifying battle was just the best damned gunfight they'd ever seen. When Junior panicked and bolted from his foxhole, they booed the chickenshit. When he collided with a tree in the darkness and we could distinctly hear the sickening thud, they laughed. I think the laughter hadn't yet subsided when the dark figure bayoneted Junior in the chest. I heard a groan pass through the audience at this moment, but it wasn't a groan at the horror of his death: It was a complaint at having been brought down from the high comedy of Junior's flight. It was a groan more grotesque than the bayonetting. But all was well when the wounded Charlie Sheen and his buddy were medivacked from the jungle. The audience bolted happily from the theater once they had that good news. A happy ending. The hero lived. That's all that matters because we are each the hero of our own story.

"Those people who laughed," said Chris as we left the theater, "they weren't really paying attention."

He's an awfully sweet kid. I think he meant to comfort me.

— Stephen Peters

In this excerpt, we see a father trying to communicate with his son. It seems that the son already knows the message he's trying to get across. But the father is changing his own story by talking with his son. He will probably have to wait and see which story his son will claim.

In terms of writing, what we notice in this excerpt is that the writer takes a long time to tell the story. This is one of the differences between story telling and fiction — the pacing. In story telling, we keep moving along, covering lots of territory with a minimum of details. The action moves us along. In fiction, we take a more leisurely pace, describe the scene, and let the characters develop. We're not in as much of a hurry to reach a conclusion.

And that brings us to the last section of this chapter.

Moving from Story to Fiction

If you like the writing you've done in this chapter, you might want to explore more complex story telling. Moving from stories to short stories, memoirs, novellas, and novels involves expanding the story to include elements that make a story dramatic and immediate:

- Description
- Dialogue
- Characterization

You also need to consider complication, climax, and resolution. These are all literary terms which refer to the techniques that make a story richer. Of course, you may have already been using these techniques naturally as you worked through this chapter. To develop this aspect of your writing, you could take a class in fiction writing. You could also develop your skills by trying out some of the following exercises. We only have space in this book to touch on some of the techniques fiction writers use. You can try out these exercises, suggested by Stephen Peters' work with students, and see if you like them.

Changing My Story

Use Stephen's story about seeing *Platoon* as a model. Describe yourself at a time when you were engaged in an activity that goes against the grain of the values of your family of origin. You are trying to change your story by behaving in a new way. Put another person in the story with you. Let this person be out of synch with you. Tell what happens. Go somewhere. Have a conversation. Take your time describing your surroundings. Don't tell your whole life, just this one hour. This can be a true story or one that you would like to have happen sometime in the future. You can make up a conversation that has not yet happened.

Changing the Family Story

Go back to your family stories and find the one that seems to have been told the most or affected you the most. Go back to where you were as a child the first time you heard the story. Describe the scene. Use your five senses and try to find in your memory one detail for each sense: food cooking, the taste of supper, music in the background, noise, the touch of the rug on your elbow. Now recall the person telling the story. Have the story come out of that person's mouth. Describe the person. Then put in as many details as you can about you — how old you were, what you were wearing, where you were sitting. What did you think of the story when you first heard it? What did you think it meant? What was the message?

When you are done writing this scene, look on the scene as the adult you are now and try to discover the storyteller's motivation in the telling of this particular anecdote. Was it about the glories of war, and consequently the true meaning of

masculinity? Was it about true love? Cleanliness is next to god-
liness? Was it about the work ethic?

Becoming a Character out of the Oral Tradition

To do this exercise, you work out of what you just wrote.
Use the same story. Only this time, you're going to make two
changes. First of all, you're going to become the original
storyteller and speak in the "I," the first person narrative voice.
Be your grandmother or be your father for an hour and talk
as they talk, saying "I."

The second change is to imagine the "I" telling the story
to a stranger, someone on a bus, or passing the time in a
waiting room at a doctor's office. What happens to the story
when it is not being told to children? Is it the same? Is it passing the same message? When you do these two exercises,
you will see the power of the story within the storyteller and
within the family.

Surrendering to Your Story

When we discover the story we can claim as the true story
of our lives, we feel a great sense of relief and serenity. When
we tell our story and we are accepted for what we are, without
judgment, we are able to begin to feel a kinship with other
people, as one AA person put it, "part of the human race."

You may discover that story telling opens you to qualities
you've always desired to have: curiosity, connection, and loving kindness.

We'll close this chapter with the reflections about the story
telling process by an AA member who is a published fiction
writer.

Writing, more often than not, is a lesson in humility.

> Time and again there is that which I want to express,
> something looming, divine, or just unaccountably sad,
> and then there is me, pretty unclear how to even begin.

What I want to express may be magic, but the writing is not. Writing is tooling and working day after day with my limited faculties of words and image trying to approximate a beauty that I've taken into my heart. It's going away from it, coming back to it, trying to see how it reads after some separateness....

The hardest thing about writing is being unable to express what I so passionately want to express. And yet this is what I face every day of the process, every day that I'm still "reaching." I have to be willing to take all the steps in the progression, some of them awkward, some of them encouraging. In fact, that I *am* taking them has become my source of joy. I have the faith that the steps *do*, small as they are, come to beauty.

— Mary L.

CHAPTER 9

Fireflies in a Jar: Writing Poetry

> *You can't do feminine without masculine. You can't do stars without the void. You can't do light without darkness.*
> — Paula Gunn Allen

Like fireflies, or lightning bugs, poems light up the night. Poetry always has the sense of a flash of inspiration. It can capture the moments of our lives that hold significance. The moment we cherish may be a special insight, a feeling shared with another person, a new thought that brings serenity, or a long-forgotten memory that awakens joy. A memory that brings pain may be captured in a poem and then be released.

Like fireflies, poems light up the night. We don't hold on to poems the way we hold on to novels (or the way novels hold on to us). When we unscrew the metal lid of the glass jar, we release the fireflies to the night, and in a similar way, when we write a poem and experience that flash, we can let it go.

A Native American poem from 1821 expresses this idea eloquently.

> What is life:
> It is the flash of a firefly
>   in the night.
> It is the breath of a buffalo

in the winter.
It is the shadow
which runs across the grass
and loses itself in the sunset.

— Crowfoot

Although many people say they are fearful of learning how to write poems, what we have discovered is that most people have written a poem somewhere along the way, maybe a love poem for Valentine's Day, poems of grief, or private poems for birthdays and graduations. Poetry *is* a shared tradition for most of us.

Many people in recovery go through other intense transitions, such as divorce or depression. Often, when this is happening, people start writing poems without ever consciously intending to do so. Poems just start bursting out. Why is this? Poems come to people at times of intense change because poems are a most intense way to express and capture the experience of our feelings.

Sometimes people who suddenly start writing are surprised not simply because the poems are coming out, but surprised because the words are coming out in a shape, a condensed lump. And then comes the question, "Is this a poem. What is a poem?"

The glib answer to this question is that you've written a poem when the words don't go all the way to the right margin of the paper. But our favorite definition, and the one easiest to understand, comes from Emily Dickinson.

If I read a book and it makes my whole body so cold no fire can ever warm me, I know that is poetry. If I feel physically as if the top of my head were taken off, I know that is poetry. These are the only ways I know it. Is there any other way?

— Emily Dickinson

We can trust our bodies to let us know when we're in touch with powerful poems.

The poems we've chosen to look at in this chapter are the ones that have been most helpful for people going through change. But they are by no means the only kind of poems that might be helpful. The world is full of wonderful poems.

In this chapter, we'll look at four kinds of poems.

- Poems of Reflection
- List Poems
- Chants
- Poems with Metaphors

Poems of Reflection

Sometimes when we reflect on an important time in our lives and write down our thoughts, our writing has a sense of wholeness, even as it is being written. It shapes itself into a poem. It centers on an important scene, a turning point, a moment of insight.

When we write a poem like this, about a significant moment, we need to use our skills of observing and describing. We also think and reflect on what we have observed. We may ask questions or make a statement about the experience we are describing.

Let's look at a poem that reflects a moment in one man's life. This poem is by the poet James Wright.

A BLESSING

Just off the highway to Rochester, Minnesota,
Twilight bounds softly forth on the grass.
And the eyes of those two Indian ponies
Darken with kindness.
They have come gladly out of the willows
To welcome my friend and me.
We step over the barbed wire into the pasture
Where they have been grazing all day, alone.

They ripple tensely, they can hardly contain their
   happiness
That we have come.
They bow shyly as wet swans. They love each other.
There is no loneliness like theirs.
At home once more,
They begin munching the young tufts of spring in the
   darkness.
I would like to hold the slenderer one in my arms,
For she was walked over to me
And nuzzled my left hand.
She is black and white,
Her mane falls wild on her forehead,
And the light breeze moves me to caress her long ear
That is delicate as the skin over a girl's wrist.
Suddenly I realize
That if I stepped out of my body I would break
Into blossom.

— James Wright

The writer stays with the physical details of his description
until the last two lines of the poem, and then he lets you know
how this experience affected him. What did you think of the
ending? He doesn't explain his feeling, he describes it. He compares himself to blossoming creation. What do you picture from
his words? An apple tree? A field of red poppies? What feelings do you take away from this poem? Relaxation? Breathless-
ness? Joy? Oneness with nature?

We learn what we like to write about by noticing what we
like in other people's poems. What do you see in this poem?
What detail do you like the best? We can see the horses moving,
for the writer tells us what they're doing, what color they are.

Now we'd like you to go back and look at the poem and see
how the writer has set up the lines and line breaks. *Line breaks*
refers to where one line of poetry ends and the next line begins.
The best way to see how a writer is handling the line breaks
is to read the poem out loud. Try doing this now. In this poem,

the lines follow the natural pauses of the writer's voice. There are many other ways to organize the lines in a poem, but we would like you to start out by writing lines according to your natural rhythms and pauses.

One of our students, Cynthia Olson, used James Wright's poem as a model for writing about an incredible event in her life. Her father had died and she was unable to accept his death; she was depressed. In the middle of one night, about six months after the death, she woke up wide-awake, with the absolute sense that she had to visit his grave. She got out of bed and drove to the graveyard. She describes the scene, with the same step-by-step detail that James Wright uses. Only gradually do we comprehend what is happening at the grave.

> Standing over Papa's fresh grave,
> tears blur BELOVED HUSBAND AND FATHER
> on the flat brass plate.
> The orange sun suddenly melts,
> spilling hot orange liquid
> from the blue September sky.
> . . . .
>
> Standing over Papa's fresh grave
> voices begin whispering, chanting
> sweet and light, helium thin and playful.
> A ritual chant, but not of death.
> The sound of a thousand fragile wings
> descending, then rising.
> So many tiny voices lighter than breath,
> singing the secret direction of the journey,
> lifting me out of the tomb, up into the orange sky.
> Is this my sign, Papa?
>
> Flying over Papa's fresh grave
> grief's fist is opened,
> releasing me to wings of rapture
> and the journey's slow dance.

I am carried on the wind of tiny breath,
a pulse so delicate, life so strong.
Protected from death by an army of Monarchs,
on their meandering journey home.
Now Papa's spirit has an orange glow.

— Cynthia Olson

The poem represents a turning point in her life, one of those fabulous moments when everything, for a split second, is clear. The epiphany is represented by this cloud of Monarchs rising from the graveyard.

The poem includes colors and sounds; the voices "helium thin and playful." It includes thoughts of the woman, asking questions and then moving into a resolution with the words, "grief's fist is opened."

We also notice that Cynthia takes her time in the poem. The line breaks follow the rhythm of the speaking voice. The poem uses verbs in the present tense; that is, the poem sounds like it is happening right now. The present tense gives us a sense of immediacy.

Now we'd like you to try writing a poem like this. Make a list of moments in your life that were turning points. Now focus on a turning point that you can recall in detail! Maybe you'll think of a time when a connection to animals gave you a great sense of peace and joy, or a time you were with a close friend. Think back to a time when you felt you had been given a blessing.

Now start writing. Write through the moment, step-by-step. Cynthia says, "All I did was write what happened." That may be, but it takes trust, sometimes, to let ourselves simply write what happened without elaborating, explaining, adding on. There is a place in our writing world for elaboration, but simple description is also a gift. Let the words flow out.

When you have written at least a page describing the experience, stop and look over what you've written. Then read it out loud to yourself. You can make slash marks on the paper where you think you'd like to make a line break. The slash is the symbol poets use to indicate line breaks. Have you described the scene with sensory details — sounds, colors, textures? Have you included one of your thoughts that expresses the experience in a fresh way, like "grief's fist is opened"? Don't explain what the scene means; rather, find one abstract statement about it that comes naturally out of the details. You may end up with a question, a surprise. For example, one woman, Kathleen S., a year into recovery, wrote a poem that describes the cat she got when she was released from the hospital. The poem ends with a revelation that surprises her:

> How did I know that
> listening to you,
> that watching you,
> holding you
> would be a way
> to care for me?
>
> — Kathleen S.

The three poems we've discussed show how we can reflect on our spiritual insights. Each flash, like a firefly, is another step in spiritual growth. There are strong feelings in these poems, but also a quietness of spirit.

Reflecting on Painful Memories

Poems of reflection can be used to write about painful memories, as well as joyful moments. In this section, we'll look at the work of writers who write about their childhood with the intention of seeing something clearly that they could not see before.

There is great healing in describing a painful time as it existed for us. We validate our experience by relating the facts of an event *as we experienced it*.

Why is writing about the past helpful to the writer? We all have a need to state our experience in order to heal. We may need to tell the truth about family secrets. The addiction process could be called "The Long Forgetfulness." There is something about addiction that continues to keep making us forget things we need to remember. Writing helps us remember what we already know. When we get it down on paper, we "get it." We have it there so that when we forget again, we can come back and read what we wrote. We can say, "I write the poems I need to read."

The poet Jill Breckenridge has written poems about growing up in an alcoholic family. In an essay about her poems, she mentions her reason for writing about the past.

> Unlike camp survivors who must join a group in order to survive, the children of violent and alcoholic families may be totally isolated. The worst damage they suffer is on the level of connection — connection to themselves, to others, and to the spiritual life that can heal and guide them on their journey.
>
> Regaining this connection is where writing, and the sharing of writing, plays a crucial role. The first time I read the poem "Bottled" to several hundred people at a Loft benefit, I was petrified . . . . Months after the reading, people revealed that their mother was alcoholic, or their father, or brother . . . .
>
> Writing poetry helps me heal, returns the life of the spirit, which was not dead, only wounded.
>
> — Jill Breckenridge

Let's turn to one of Jill Breckenridge's poems, a poem called "My Mother's Hands." In this poem, the writer has gone back into her memory and really looked at her mother, as if she had a camera. Read the poem and see if you can visualize with her.

MY MOTHER'S HANDS

Puffy as blown-up rubber gloves,
each stubby finger groped
for some happiness she never

grasped. Those hands forecast
her disposition by the violence
of their shaking. When she'd
been drinking, they flopped
around her lap like wet birds.
After her death, the jeweler near
her office said she came in
every day during lunch hour
and tried on rings, stretching out
her fingers to look at the glimmer
of rubies and emeralds she never
owned, gems to refresh hands
tired from typing insurance forms
turned in by the rich claiming
money for their stolen goods,
hands I give this poem to,
bloated swans, chapped lily-red.

— Jill Breckenridge

What do we see in this poem? We see details of touch and color: *puffy, lily-red, bloated.* We see size and shape: *stubby fingers, blown-up rubber gloves.* We see movement by the comparison of the hands to flopping wet birds. We see the contrast of poverty and wealth. We see a lot in twenty lines. Even though the writer doesn't say how she's feeling, we may feel sadness at the end of the poem when she says she dedicates the poem to her mother's hands.

This close attention to detail, which requires the emotional stability *to stay in the scene* and look at what you see, holds a poem like this together. This poem can be a helpful model for you in writing about your childhood.

We want to show you now how another writer, Patricia Simons, used Jill Breckenridge's poem as a model for writing about her own childhood. This poem follows the close attention to detail but adds a new angle: after a while, it sounds like the writer is speaking in a child's voice, the voice she had in her childhood. The choice to talk like the child you once were is a powerful way to unlock memories.

MY MOTHER'S HANDS

My mother's hands have long red fingernails
She keeps them painted,
Spends hours changing shades.

My mother's hands have a Lucky in them
Or a lighter, there are nicotine stains
On her middle finger. She sits and clicks
The lighter while she talks, her cigarettes
Have bright red lipstick.

My mother's hands are small
Heavy-veined; when I was young,
They came at me like eagle talons swooping
Across my face, or they threw
Objects at me from across the room.
Sometimes she would balance
Her white plastic hairbrush
Between one hand and the other.

My mother's hands have strength to push me
Into locked rooms, dark closets.
They scrape me, go into my secret places,
My legs flow red, she smiles —
Her fingernails and lips match my blood.

They tell me my mother's hands
Are now dead.
In the seconds before I wake
they still come at me...
— Patricia Simons

Let yourself be in the poem and feel the impact of the mother's hands on the child. The adult writer does not state her feelings directly, but the details speak for themselves. What feelings do you get from the poem? Because the writer does not name the feelings, we are *not* limited to having only one feeling in response to the poem. We may feel sadness, terror, anger, or despair when we read the poem. We are free to have our own feeling response, separate from the writer.

Writing as If You Had a Camera

We mentioned that Jill Breckenridge's poem looked closely at her mother, as if she had a camera. Other writers use the idea of a camera to describe an entire scene. They hold the scene in memory, freeze frame. Still others who are doing work on family of origin issues find it useful to go through old family photographs and write about one photograph, or a scene suggested by a photograph.

The next poem about a childhood scene combines the sense of a camera with yet another strategy: writing in the third person. We talked about this strategy in the chapter, Walking in Someone Else's Shoes. It is a useful technique when we are writing about painful memories. The third person automatically gives us some distance that we may need to even begin to write about pain. There is a time when we need to say "I," but the third person is a safe way to begin.

This poem, "Touching," by the writer John Caddy; it's from his book, *The Color of Mesabi Bones.*

TOUCHING

The clothesline hums with fear.
The boy is watching from the corner of the house.
The man is going to beat the dog,
who cringes at the end of the rope,
ears flat and withers shrinking,
who can never believe this is happening.

All of them are living in their throats.
The man is red, the boy is pale.
Both are trying not to cry.

The boy is caught within another laying on of hands, at
the cabin when they cleared the brush
and the wheelbarrow piled with branches
was too much for him, when the birch turned switch
and laid open his skin.

The dog presents his throat and yelps again.
The boy grips his forearm where
the scars lie white across the tan.

— John Caddy

We notice the incredible tension in this scene, "Both are
trying not to cry." John Caddy stays within the literal description to capture the tension. Because he doesn't *tell* us what
to feel, we are open to many feelings: we may feel pity for
the dog; outrage at the father's behavior. Or, our attention may
focus on the child and we may feel a deep sorrow. We may
feel admiration for the adult writer, the man, who is expressing such vulnerable feelings about the father-son relationship
and masculinity.

To write a poem like this one, go through your old family
photographs. Pick one that suggests a scene of strong feelings,
either the scene in the picture or a memory suggested by the
picture. Simply describe what you see. Write as if you had a
camera. Be as dispassionate as if you were drawing a blueprint.
This will help you get it out on paper.

For Those Working on Family of Origin Issues

We would like to pause for a moment and comment on the
experiences of some people who begin to work on family of
origin issues. Some people discover that their childhood is a
blank. How can you write about the family album if you've
blanked out everything around it? One suggestion is to start

writing the questions you have, about the pictures, about your own blank spots, or about any objects you have from childhood. You might begin with one toy, like Jodie M., who has started her family origin work, after six years in recovery, working through her cocaine and dependency. One day at an antique and collectible show she noticed a doll exactly like the one she had when she was eight years old, Chatty Cathy. She had forgotten about her! She is now writing out her questions, asking her doll for assistance.

> I look at you closely, hoping I will remember a piece
> — something. You must have been my best friend. The
> one who knew. The one who played with Jodie. What
> was it like there in my room? What secrets did I tell you?
> What was played out?
>
> — Jodie M.

It's too soon for Jodie to know if her questions will lead to a poem, a story, an essay, but her questions will lead her to a form. Many writers have fashioned wonderful poems that consist entirely of questions.

Jodie's questions lead us to another common experience of people doing family of origin work. Often, a person starts out writing in one form, and the volcano of memories suddenly shifts the writing into another form. If this happens, don't be alarmed. Shifts in the earth's plates are part of nature. One person who experienced this shift is Merica Palen, a writer in the Adult Children of Alcoholics Program. She had been writing poetry for over twenty years. When she started doing her family of origin work, she suddenly found herself writing about her childhood home, in prose.

> I smell cigarette smoke and liquor and I hear a heated
> argument. I see my father standing, face red, eyes bulg-
> ing, spit spraying out of his mouth. Fists clenching,
> directing white hot words at my mother . . . . Now her
> head and eyes are lowered, . . . her hands lay limp in

her lap and she mumbles. Her complexion is yellow
with too much alcohol. . . .

— Merica Palen

You can see that the description technique is similar, whether
you are writing in poetry or prose. If you find prose easier for
childhood memories, then write in prose. Turn to Chapter
Eight, Telling Our Stories, and work there. You can come back
to poetry when it's time.

We want to repeat our belief that this kind of writing is so
powerful that most people need lots of support when they are
doing it. Make sure you find the support of an appropriate
counselor or group if you discover, through your writing,
memories that you didn't know you had. The words *recover,*
uncover, and *discover* are close to one another. Sometimes we
discover something we're not sure we want to know. When
this happens, support of other people is crucial for us to maintain our mental health and our spiritual connection.

Chants and List Poems

Chants and list poems rely more on the rhythm and play
of words against each other than other poems do. The rhythm
often suggests a drumbeat, a heartbeat, an insistence. These
poems are a channel for strong feelings.

Recovery work lets out lots of feelings: anger, grief, sorrow,
passion, shame, ecstasy, relief, fear. All these feelings can be
channeled into list poems and chants. The *form* of these poems
lets strong feelings flow through them.

The difference between the two forms is like the difference
between an arrow and a circle. *List poems* list one thing after
another in a fashion that builds in intensity toward a final tar-
get, like an arrow in flight. *Chants* are like a circle. They have
at least one line that repeats over and over throughout the
poem. The poem ends where it begins; yet each repetition
encloses and gathers in more information, more feeling.

We'll look at each of these two kinds of poems separately, because even though they are similar, each requires a different kind of approach for you as you write.

List Poems

List poems present endless possibilities for us as writers. We've already talked about the fact that since everyone has made grocery lists, we already know we can write lists. Basically, a list poem consists of adding on, adding on, adding on. The lines add on and add up to an increasing intensity of thought and feeling. The poem ends with the *thwack* of an arrow hitting the bull's eye.

Another word for a list poem is a *catalogue*. The American writer most famous for cataloguing is Walt Whitman. His book-length poem, *Leaves of Grass*, contains many catalogues of people and places he loves, across the width and breadth of the United States.

What we didn't talk about in the chapter on lists is how to go about transforming a list into a list poem. The main trick to making a list poem lies in how it's organized. We'll look at some of the ways writers have dealt with organizing. There are three ways we'll consider here.

- List Poems Are an Open Channel to Timeless Feelings
- List Poems Track the Passage of Time
- List Poems Follow Natural Shapes

List Poems Are an Open Channel to Timeless Feelings

The first poem we'll talk about is "Fear," by Raymond Carver.

FEAR

Fear of seeing a police car pull into the drive.
Fear of falling asleep at night.
Fear of not falling asleep.
Fear of the past rising up.

Fear of the present taking flight.
Fear of the telephone that rings in the dead of the night.
Fear of electrical storms.
Fear of the cleaning woman who has a spot on her cheek!
Fear of dogs I've been told won't bite.
Fear of anxiety.
Fear of having to identify the body of a dead friend.
Fear of running out of money.
Fear of having too much, though people will not believe this.
Fear of psychological profiles.
Fear of being late and fear of arriving before anyone else.
Fear of my children's handwriting on envelopes.
Fear they'll die before I do, and I'll feel guilty.
Fear of having to live with my mother in her old age,
        and mine.
Fear of confusion.
Fear this day will end on an unhappy note.
Fear of waking up to find you gone.
Fear of not loving and fear of not loving enough.
Fear that what I love will prove lethal to those I love.
Fear of death.
Fear of living too long.
Fear of death.
    I've said that.

— Raymond Carver

Take a minute to let this poem settle in and then consider
which of these fears you identify with. Which fears would be
on your list? Everyone has fears.

We'd like you to get out paper and pencil and set the timer
for three minutes. See how many fears you can list in three
minutes! Be as childish and irrational as you need to be. Write
down the most trivial fears you have. Write down fears you
used to have and you think went away — but you're not sure.

Did you fill up the page? If you need more time, take more
time. Most people can get out about thirty fears in three

minutes. Fear is big these days. We may all have fears, and channeling them through a poem is one way of releasing them.

Look at your list and see if there is a theme running through the list. In Raymond Carver's poem, there are many images of death. We also see a concern for losing loved ones. Our students who have made their own lists have discovered other themes. Fears about our children's safety. Fears about winter; cars breaking down. Fears about loneliness. Fears about money. Teenagers often list the fear of getting mugged, fear of zits, fear of nuclear war — usually in that ranking. If you find one theme, you might stop and add more lines that deal with this theme. Do that now.

Now let's look at how Raymond organized his lines. We see that there is a rhythm to the poem, alternating between flowing lines and abrupt, cut-short lines. We see that he uses some abstract words like *confusion* and *anxiety*, but that he always follows them with specific details. The poem is packed with specific details. It swings back and forth between abstraction and specificity.

What else do you see? The details are arranged in such a way that they are pairs of fears, such as fear of falling asleep versus fear of not falling asleep. We think that these opposites, combined with the growing sense of death, work to give an overwhelming sense of dread.

So the choice here, for you, is to write a poem like this. You may organize your list around a theme, around opposites, or both.

Here is the way one student handled this writing exercise. He didn't want to work with opposites. He wanted to work with one theme: his fear of his wife drinking again. He took one line from his original list and wrote a second list of all the details that surrounded this fear, "fear of your drinking."

KENTUCKY REEL

Fear of that poison that made Kentucky famous
burning down your yearning lips
coursing through your sober veins.

Fear of that wildfire of fermented yeasts and grain
raging up your spine
tripping sensors
searing neural cells and codes
to make you a wasteland.

Our fears entangle to weave a web of broken promises,
a crazy quilt to cover nights of winter madness,
when we toe a dizzy circle
dance to Eighty Proof time.

Our tongues play tricks when words
lash like rocks flung out in haste
when reason fails, fingers point, excuses bend,
and morning's numb memory recalls a world that wasn't.

Fear of spinning freefalls
reaching for cords and hooks,
a red button to push
before the crash.

Fear of fifteen straight years going down the drain,
like the bottle I poured out before your eyes one
    angry night.

                              — David W.

   Now, with all these possibilities in mind, take out a fresh
piece of paper and make a list poem about fear. You can start
with the list you made during the three minute timed writing. Add to it, rearrange it, play with it.

List Poems Track the Passage of Time

The list poems we just looked at can exist free of time and space. But the same form, the list, can also track events in the order that they happened. This is called *chronological order*. We can make a list of major events in our lives, milestones, turning points, and summarize in this way our entire life on one sheet of paper. This kind of poem is like a time line.

Some Native American people, and others around the world, used list poems as a verbal way of keeping track of time before they had writing. As a group, they named each year by its most significant event. This oral tradition named every single year. When they named the year, they tried to use visual language so that there would be a picture of the year to help everyone remember. For example, the year 1988 could be called "The Year of the Drought." But which words would give the year a picture name? We could say, "The Year We Waded Across the Mississippi."

This process of naming the years is called *Winter Count*. The writer, Susan Marie Swanson, and other writers, have used this form to write poems about their own lives. The poem may focus on winters, on summers, or on the years with all the seasons.

Here is a poem by a beginning writer, remembering other summers. The student, Kevin J. Peterson, worked on finding an image for every year of his life but then chose only the strongest images.

SUMMER SONNET MINUS TWO

summer turned 8
                on the red Schwinn birthday
summer turned 13
                while delivering the big news, Bobby
                    Kennedy

summer turned 15

    on a bike without brakes, rolling
       marijuana

summer turned 18

    for the Cool Hand Luke, hero
       in the class of drifters

summer turned 19

    the day I cut *jazz* in the grass

summer turned 20

    in Hare's Hideout at the bottom of
       Payne Avenue

summer turned 21

    in the slaughter house singing

summer turned 23

    walking drunks through midnight halls
       of detox

summer turned 26

    selling Shaklee door to door

summer turned 30

    in a house with golf clubs and a garage
       door opener

summer turned 31

    my mother said *you're getting old*

summer turned 34

    painting a house in the sun
                — Kevin J. Peterson

There's so much life in this poem! We see a wide range of memories from one man's life. We see private memories, and memories from the larger, shared culture. We see a suburban house, and images of the inner city. We see someone smoking dope, and someone working at detox — the same person at different times in his life. We see a man singing in the slaughterhouse — why he doesn't say; it's a mystery.

To write a "counting" poem, start by making a list of strong images from your life. Write down the first image that comes to mind. Then add a few. You don't have to use the first image that pops in your head, but it is often the strongest. You may think that a poem about every year of your life is a bit much. So follow your unconscious. Record the years that leap out at you. Try for twelve, as Kevin did.

The next step in writing this poem is condensing your words so that each year only takes one line. That's all the space you get. The image has to be short, direct, vivid. Each line gives us a picture. You may have to let certain memories float up, but you can work slowly. Trust that they will float up.

List Poems Follow Natural Shapes

After any trauma, any loss, any life change or illness, we suddenly turn around one day, and say, "Pinch me, I can't believe I'm alive." Writing about our physical body is one way to welcome ourselves back to the land of the living, for even if the trauma was emotional, not physical, our bodies suffer during trauma. We ignore them. It is healing to acknowledge physical beauty.

You may say, "Wait a minute, there's nothing beautiful about my puffy face, my stretch marks, my skinny ribs." Maybe not. But there's more to you than the physical-emotional wreck that you see when being critical. What about you feels good to you? The color of your hair? Hands strong enough to hold a pencil?

In the following poem, the writer, Joan Larkin, whose book *A Long Sound* offers wonderful poems about recovery and lesbian issues, uses body imagery to represent her emotional healing.

HOW THE HEALING TAKES PLACE

How the face changes, the cloud
you'd skim from a pot of lentils
comes clear, how the gaze
comes clear as honey when you heat it,

how the eyes surrender their fear,
dark lake of beach plums
boiled for jam. How flesh

yields new flesh, lips
softening like soaked beans.
How the puffed skin settles,
dough becomes bread,
its brown, delicate grain.
How the dead hair — that mouse,
matted and stiff in the trap —
grows sleek again. How the thoughts,

like black ants going
and coming from the mouse's corpse,
go slower. How the torn mind
puts forth tendrils.
How the gray house of the lungs,
frayed and weather-beaten,
fills with moist breath.
How the breath brings healing

to all parts of the body.
To the salt rivers of blood,
to the many-tiered skeleton,
to the breast, beaded and creased,
humming like wings in the jewel-weed,
to the softening belly,
to the thick, unfurling petals of the sex.

How everything speaks —
hands unclenching —
heart.
How the belly will lift its flat
stone, the tears roll
stones from entrances.

— Joan Larkin

This poem is full of details from the natural world. The writer brings in images from nature — the river, the beach plums, the hummingbird — and all these images give a rich life to the healing body. The writer compares the body to other things in order to get across exactness. For example, when she wants to say that her hair had been dull and lifeless, she doesn't say "dull and lifeless," she says it was like a mouse caught in a trap. Comparing one thing to another is a useful process for description. If you look back, you'll see that James Wright also uses comparisons to enrich his descriptions of the ponies.

When we first read this poem, we felt awash in the rich detail and didn't even think about how it was organized. We loved it for the detail, and the powerful message of healing. But then we noticed the organization and that added another dimension. The details are arranged, in a list, in the natural order of the human body, starting with the face. This human ordering gives the list a shape, a wholeness.

We'd like you to write now a poem in praise of your body. For a first step, do this: get out a fresh sheet of paper. Draw a line down the middle. At the top of one column, write "Body," and at the top of the other column, write "Compared To." Now list the body parts you like in the first column. The second column will take more time. Find things in the natural world to really convey the color or feel of your body. For example, let's say that "eyes" is first on your list. If you want to depict their color, you might say, "dark blue, the lake after sundown."

The second step is arranging the list in a shape. You can do what Joan Larkin did and work from the face down. Or there may be another order that will follow the human body. You might start with the hands and work to the inside of the body, to the heart. Or start with the feet and work up. You could work from the inside out.

Writers in Twelve Step programs have said that they often start writing and don't think about which Step the writing is connected to until after they are finished. The Twelve Steps form a structure that allows a person to learn how to love others

and love the self. Loving yourself includes loving your body.
It is difficult to see which Step has to do with physical health,
as it can affect and be affected by all the Steps. But the image
of healing in Joan Larkin's poem resonates with Step Twelve,
practicing "these principles in all our affairs." If you want to
do more with Step Twelve, write a poem like Joan Larkin's.

Another way to work with a poem like Joan Larkin's is to
think of other natural shapes that could provide the organizing principle for a list. You might think of a landscape, the
universe, or a backyard as a spatial arrangement the poem
could model itself after. Poet Kate Green has written a wonderful poem, organized around a house. We include it for your
enjoyment, not as a writing exercise; you could, however, write
one like it, if you want to.

DON'T MAKE YOUR LIFE TOO BEAUTIFUL

Don't fix the three-foot hole in the plaster
over the stairway.
Don't sweep up the tiny specks of white
that gather in dust like stars.
Leave the hole under the fence
the dog dug in the marigolds
that never flowered.
You can look for hours at the pile
of shingles your neighbor ripped off his roof
and left to mold the green summer
with plenty of dark underneath for the beetles
and the worms to damp in.
Leave the rocks imbedded in odd places in the lawn.
And the black locust you cut down year after year —
you can let it become a tree after all,
towering thorns over the lilies and the peonies.
Look out the cracked window —
that broccoli just kept blooming
until the ice came down

and made us bend over our hands
in search of something we held and lost.
Leave it all exactly as it is.
There are heartaches enough to live for.
Leave the old worn boots stacked in the hall,
the rotten mattress in the flagstone basement.
Live out your ecstasy on earth
amid the flaking patio stones,
the boarded-up back door
and the rusty car.

— Kate Green

Chants

Chants, like list poems, have a strong rhythm. They differ from Lists in that they have a repeating line which makes the poem move like a circle rather than an arrow. List poems build in intensity to the ending, while chants could go on forever, as they indeed do in some forms of spiritual practice.

Chants, as some poems, end where they begin. The poem turns on a word or a phrase that repeats and turns. Each turn reveals more. Each turn layers more. Each turn encloses more as it moves, like moving through a spiral, collecting and moving on, just as a gyroscope includes more and more space as it moves. A chant is like weaving May Pole ribbons. It is like turning a faceted gem. It is like lacquering a box to a deep luster. The voice in a chant is insistent; it may be obsessed and insistent, or lulling and insistent, or angry and insistent — but always insistent.

Chants channel our feelings, whatever they are — joy, anguish, serenity — through the power of repetition and rhythm. The Irish people call spoken anguish *keening*. Wailing. We've heard of the Wailing Wall in Jerusalem. We don't have one here in this country. There's hardly anywhere a person can go and wail. Maybe to their car. Maybe to the bathroom. Maybe to a support group. Our lack of opportunity for wailing makes our writing about grief all the more meaningful.

Our first example of a chant is one of the first poems written by a student, Elizabeth Johnson. Her eighteen-year-old daughter was killed in a car accident, and the grief over this loss was the volcano that lead her to poetry.

THE WOMAN WHO WAILED

the woman who wailed
  in the grass, in the spring
  wailed on the hill
  on her knees, in the spring
the woman who wailed
  with the sound from her knees
  with the sound coming out
  from her belly and knees
the sound ripping out
  spilling life on the ground
  on the blanket of sod
  newly placed, on the earth
wailed at the grass
  laid across the bare earth
  fit into the rectangle
  cut in the ground
tore with her fingernails
  into the roots
  of the barrier grass
  between her and her child
crouched on the hill
  with the rushes of sound
  choking on phlegm
  in the wails in the grass

the woman who wailed
   unable to stand
   grinding the daffodils
   under her hand
the woman who wailed
the woman who waited.

         — Elizabeth Johnson

What we see in this poem is a person honoring her own grief. The repetition of the phrase "the woman who wailed" is the phrase that centers the poem. We see that the other lines in the poem have to do with very specific actions, such as "tore with her fingernails," and "choking on phlegm." We also see that the writer has chosen to write about herself in the third person, in the same way as John Caddy.

If you want to write a poem like this, think about a time you were in extreme emotion. Sit down, go on automatic pilot, and write out all the things you did, all the details about the world around you, what touched your body — all the internal body reactions. The crucial elements in this kind of poem are the actions and physical sensations alternating with the abstractness of the repeating line. The writer is naming the sensations, not the feelings. We feel the feelings from watching the actions.

After you have written on automatic pilot, go back and look for a repeating line. It might be, "The man who sat in his car and cried." It's okay to take the line Elizabeth Johnson used and try it in your own poem. There's a saying that goes around writers' circles. "Good poets borrow; great poets steal." This is not the same as plagiarism. If you see a phrase that you have the sense to know is great, when you take it and put it in your own poem, you will transform it and make it yours.

Once you've found your repeating line, go back and combine the chant line with the details. Work by talking out loud. Keep talking until you hear your own insistent rhythm coming out.

Chants can also be used to channel intense positive feelings, such as serenity, joy, lovingness, letting go, and a sense of oneness with the universe. In fact, some of these positive feelings are vague and hard to name. The rhythm of a chant helps make them real. In the following poem, Nancy Paddock writes about one way of letting go by getting grounded (centered). Notice, as you read, how she uses the same strategies as Elizabeth Johnson, alternating the abstract chant line and the specific details.

LIE DOWN

Lie down with your belly to the ground,
like an old dog in the sun. Smell
the green of the cloverleaf, feel
the damp earth through your clothes, let
an ant wander the uncharted territory
of your skin. Lie down
with your belly to the ground. Melt into
the earth's contours like a harmless snake.
All else is mere bravado.
Let your fists open into useless tendrils.
Let your mind resolve itself
in a tangle of grass.
Lie down with your belly
to the ground, flat out, on ground level.
Prostrate yourself
before the soil you will someday enter.
Stop doing.
Stop judging, fearing, trying.
This is not dying, but the way to live
in a world of change and gravity.
Let go. Let your burdens drop.

Let your grief-charge bleed off
into the ground. Lie down
with your belly to the ground
and then rise up
with the earth still in you.

— Nancy Paddock

Chants and Step Three

Letting go is a difficult process. Most people describe a desire
to let go and yet feel an internal resistance to the process.
Chants help deal with this resistance with their gentle repetition. Make a list of all the phrases you can think of that would
go with Step Three.

* Let go
* Let it go
* Let it flow
* Turn it over
* In the hands of God
* All is well

Make the list as long as you like. Now write out all the things
you could do that give you a sense of letting go. Maybe, like
Nancy Paddock, you like to go outdoors to let go. Other ways
that people find helpful are: taking a bath, running, making
something with your hands. Make a list of actions that you
know help you. Then write out some of these actions with your
repeating line. And *voila!* You will have a chant.

Poems with Metaphors

When we say, "My depression was a huge pit," we're making a metaphor. When we say, "Hope is grass pushing up
through a concrete sidewalk," we're making a metaphor.
Metaphors convey a feeling without stating it directly. This technique comes very naturally to the human mind and it is powerful in poetry.

Some people from dysfunctional families use metaphors cautiously, because they spent so many years in a fog of denial and sideways communication. These people want their writing to be based in reality. They think, *If it's depression, call it depression, not a pit.* They say that childhood was filled with situations changing unpredictably from one thing to another; consequently, what they want in their poems is for things to stay as they are. Poems are a source of grounding, a reality check, and stability. Jill Breckenridge writes, "Metaphor often disguises experience, often sings when it should shout or scream. Hidden warfare demands a witness to name it."

The advantage of metaphor is that it may help you express a feeling that eludes you in realistic description. All techniques can be useful. We suggest that you try many kinds of writing before settling on one alone. For example, you might write poems that realistically describe scenes of growing up in a dysfunctional family, and then turn to metaphor to convey the relentless terror you felt as a child.

Let's look at some metaphors about hope and recovery. Many people working on Steps Two, Three, and Eleven use metaphor to redefine their spirituality. To change, expand, and enlarge the concept of a Higher Power, many people begin by listing the many wonderful spiritual images they associate with a Higher Power: groups, nature, friends, fire, the Milky Way, the center of the earth. You can refer back to Chapter Three for another writing exercise.

Another way to work is to make a quick list of images that represent recovery for you. You may start with our list and add your own images.

Recovery is...

- a meadow surrounded by pine trees
- a bed by an open window
- the light at the end of the tunnel
- a red cardinal
- swimming in the ocean without fear

Now pick one image from your list to use for a poem. For example, if you picked the cardinal, you might write:

> Recovery is a cardinal,
> the red flash
> outside my window,
> greeting this airy room
> where the shades
> used to be pulled until
> noon.

If you want to be the cardinal yourself, imagine what you would be doing. Here's one person's short flight.

> Open to the wind
> I flew, despite sharp warnings,
> blossomed — vibrant red.
>
> — Pat Willis Vincent

If you want to learn more about writing poetry, any library has books you can use. We suggest that you look for a poem you love, and learn by using its techniques and structure. If you want to write more about dysfunctional families and addiction, you might start with books by Raymond Carver, Joan Larkin, John Caddy, Judy Grahn, Tess Gallagher, and Sharon Olds.

And so we see that our journey through this chapter has taken us from watching the fireflies to flying through the wind ourselves. We know you will continue on your journey with even more images of beauty.

CHAPTER 10

Odds and Ends: Writing, Drawings, and Documents

Odd how the creative power at once brings the whole universe to order.
— Virginia Woolf

To be surrounded by beautiful things has much influence upon the human creature: to make beautiful things has more.
— Charlotte Perkins Gilman

When we start writing, we may not realize how extensive our journey will be. One road leads to another. We may find ourselves drawn to other forms of creative expression. We may find ourselves enjoying the creative process and looking for other ways to express ourselves. We find surprises on our journey, and so we've called this chapter "Odds and Ends." It's about unexpected gifts.

In this chapter, we'll look at some creative kinds of writing, writing that begins in unusual ways, such as:

- Drawing and writing together
- Using formal language and documents for spiritual purposes
- Writing new rituals and ceremonies

As we have worked on this book, we've asked people the simple question, "What kind of writing has been most helpful to you on your spiritual journey?" Sometimes the answers are surprising, for example, when someone answers, "Doodling." These answers don't fit into the usual categories. Much of this chapter came from what other people told us.

We'll start with some of the more lighthearted suggestions and then move on to more formal suggestions.

Doodling, Shape Poems, and Calligraphy

Many people like to doodle, draw, and play with shapes. These people don't consider themselves artists, but they have fun. It's okay not to be a professional. Just as it's okay to write a lot even if you don't consider yourself a writer yet. Doodling can help us understand new concepts. It can help us discover where our unconscious thoughts and feelings are moving. After all, the charts and schemas we see in self-help books probably started with somebody sitting around doodling. If you are having trouble with a concept, a feeling, or the transition from one concept to another, try doodling. Here's an example of the doodlings of a person in Adult Children of Alcoholics struggling with feelings of emptiness.

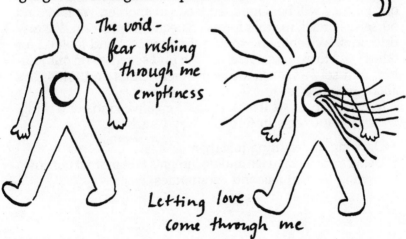

The void –
fear rushing
through me
emptiness

Letting love
come through me

Take a few minutes and try doodling. Try several different writing utensils: pencils, pens, felt tip markers. Try drawing shapes to go with a particular feeling: emptiness, love, anger, fear, isolation. After you have spent some time doodling and have made many shapes and forms, pick one to write about. For example, the doodler for the void-person, wrote the following:

> When this guy is feeling empty, boy is he empty, you can see through him, he looks like he's been shot through the guts. He's got nothing left. But that same hole, it can be so full, so filled with the winds of love.

The next example is from the work of artist, writer, and teacher, Antiga. We'd like you to go through your journals and notes and find any lines you've written that you like, words that you are really attached to. When you have identified your favorite lines, write them out in a shape that somehow suggests their meaning to you. For example, you might want to write your sentences about letting go in what you feel is the shape of the wind. If you know how to do calligraphy, you may write your words in calligraphy. An inexpensive felt marker from the drugstore can make beautiful shapes. You might also like doing the process in reverse, which involves drawing a shape in pencil first and then writing in words that fit along the lines. This is a playful and relaxing way to work with special thoughts and feelings. Here is the example from Antiga:

Health is being present to myself; being inside where disease before me; It takes me just as I am, relaxing into the journey, learning from the center of my life, being still as I am, accepting me, going with what I have, paying attention to what I don't have, learning from what I find inside. It takes me; looking for me.

— Antiga

If you enjoy this, you might enjoy these two books: *The Creative Journal,* by Lucia Capacchione, and *Drawing from the Right Side of the Brain,* by Betty Edwards.

All of your work with drawing can be connected to the Twelve Steps. Any work you are doing on the Steps may come more easily after you have expressed the feelings through art.

Cartooning

Fooling around with shapes and doodles can easily lead to cartooning. Cartoons are fun. They can be a practical way to lighten up, look at our own limitations, frustrations, and foibles. We can also lighten up our expectations of other people and the world. When we can laugh at ourselves and our perfectionism, we can move forward more easily.

You may express concerns about our culture through cartoons. Here is the work of Scott Adams, who is concerned about ecology.

— Scott J. Adams

You may not be ready to draw a whole cartoon, but you can enjoy cartooning in the following way. Cut out cartoons from the newspapers and magazines and either cut off the captions or scribble them out. Now make up your own captions. For example, if you are working on letting go of anger, you might look for characters in the cartoons who look mad, who look like they intend to stay mad. What would they be saying? What would the other characters be saying to them?

More Drawing and Writing

There are many other wonderful ways to work with drawing to center our spirit. Often, drawing will unlock our feelings in a way that lets us begin writing after we have finished drawing. At other times, writing and drawing come to us, hand in hand.

In this section, we'd like to talk about one more way of working with drawing and writing that has been helpful in recovery: drawing a mandala.

Mandalas

A *mandala* is a circle with pictures and designs inside of it. Mandalas are used to center thoughts and feelings. They appear all over the world, in all religions. Buddhists use mandalas for meditating. A mandala is the shape of the rose windows in European cathedrals. The mandala is part of Hopi sand paintings. It is also seen in the sacred circle shield of the Native Americans who lived in the Plains.

We can see the psychological basis for the power of the mandala in the work of Carl Jung. When he was working with people who'd had total personality breakdowns, he discovered that if they were given paper and pencil they would spontaneously begin to draw mandalas. Something deep within them was drawn to the comfort of the circle. During the process of therapy, Jung's clients would go on to draw many mandalas, each one different, each one bringing more integration to their lives. In this same fashion, one of our friends keeps a "Mandala Journal." When she wakes in the night with insomnia and fears, she gets up and draws for herself a new image of wholeness.

Here's how to make a mandala. Take some plain, white paper and make a circle in the middle by tracing around a plastic lid, or a plate. (Coffee can lids work fine.) If you want, you may divide the circle into four quadrants, a style used in some mandalas around the world. Now look at your circle and ask yourself which pictures and designs will give you the greatest sense of peace and serenity. Think of places you love, such as lakes or oceans; think of seasons, day and night; think of animals and creatures, rocks and cozy hide-outs. Start drawing one of your images and then follow what comes out next. You don't have to plan ahead; let yourself follow your hand. When you are done, you may add colors if you like.

— Kathleen Kruger

After you've drawn your mandala, you may write about it. Sometimes people write as though they were small enough to go into the mandala and write, starting with the words, "Inside my mandala, there are coils and bursts of lights. . ." The artist, Kathleen Kruger, who drew the mandala in this book, wrote the following thoughts about what she drew.

> This mandala is about motherhood. The child and I share the same navel at its exact center. The interwoven ribbons around the edge are my daughter's.

> The upper right represents sunlight, hope, and the future. It is all the accomplishment and joy and hope I have for my children, as they live their lives.

> The pod-like cradle in the lower right gets in a flower surrounded by vines. It represents my desire to protect and cradle my children and my visual prayer for their safety and health.

The chaos in the lower left is fear and confusion and frustration.

The baby's mouth in the upper left has two meanings for me. It is the sweetness of infancy and the continual needs of all children, sweetness and exhaustion.

And the circle returns us to sunlight.

— Kathleen Kruger

Writing in the Language of Formal Documents

When we write letters, we may feel comfortable because we already know the form of letters and can fit our thoughts into one without struggling with the form. We also have a ready-to-use form when we use the language of formal documents. We probably studied the Bill of Rights in grade school. Maybe we had to memorize the Preamble to the Constitution. We've handled many documents in adult life: birth certificates, contracts, deeds, agreements, tax forms, divorce papers. The rhythm and shape of these forms is all in our heads. The words may seem like legalese cluttering up our brains, but they are a resource for us. We can use the language of law and commerce for our spiritual growth.

We'll talk about three ways to use this language:

- Bill of Rights
- Contract with Self
- The Creative Calendar

Bill of Rights

The first example is from the Bill of Rights. Many therapists and recovery programs encourage people to write their own Bill of Rights to learn about setting healthy boundaries. When do you feel good about being open? What are you touchy about? When do you feel invaded? A Bill of Rights helps clarify this. To start your own Bill of Rights, ask yourself what you need to feel safe about, then begin with, for example, "I have the right to shut the door to my room. I have the right to expect people to knock before entering." Don't be afraid to sound childish. If you never before had the right to a shut door, now is the time to begin, even if it's a right you should have had when you were a small child. Continue with your list. You are making this list for yourself. You don't necessarily have to show it to anyone, but there will probably be surprises on it that you will want to share.

Contract with Self

Our next example is the Contract with the Self. This is an agreement made between one person and his or her self. Like affirmations, contracts with ourselves should be phrased positively, focusing on what is to occur, rather than on what we don't like or "shouldn't" do.

Using lofty and sometimes pretentious language can be fun and freeing. The weight of the words can add a sense of importance to the actions we are attempting to integrate into our lives. The process of writing in business language provides a fresh approach to working the Steps because it gives a new angle on the slogans and familiar phrases of recovery language.

Here is an example of a contract for self-care written by Cynthia Orange.

CONTRACTUAL AGREEMENT WITH SELF, INC

WHEREAS, _____, hereinafter referred to as "Party of the First Part," has demonstrated the ability to achieve and maintain a state of abstinence from _____, and;

WHEREAS, Party of the First Part continues to exhibit the requisite elements integral to successful recovery, and;

WHEREAS, Party of the First Part has furthermore expressed a willingness to advance within the personal entity heretofore known as SELF, Inc., hereinafter referred to as "Party of the Second Part";

NOW, THEREFORE, IT IS HEREIN AGREED BY AND BETWEEN THE PARTIES HERETO AS FOLLOWS;

That Party of the Second Part, in recognition of the significant achievements made by Party of the First Part in his/her position as Recovering Person, hereby promotes said Party of the First Part to the position of Business Manager. Party of the First Part agrees to undertake the following responsibilities:

1. To celebrate on an on-going basis the joy of recovery;
2. To relegate to others only those duties which are approximately theirs and to accept those responsibilities which rest solely with Party of the First Part;
3. To accept the consequences of individual actions and reactions;
4. To adopt the philosophy of SELF worth; that is, the belief that a healthy and whole individual is one who honors his or her uniqueness, accepts and forgives imperfections, understands limitations, and nurtures body, mind, and spirit on an on-going basis.
5. If, for any reason, any associate of SELF, Inc., must be let go, Party of the First Part understands that said associate is to be released with love and any and all other benefits to which said associate may be entitled.

All statements above have read and understood.

_____

Signatory: Party of the First Part

DURATION OF CONTRACT: _____ *Just for Today* _____

— Cynthia Orange

Now, we'd like you to play around with the idea of a contract with yourself. Take the five points in this contract and change them to suit your own situation. See if you can let your sense of humor come out in the legal language.

The Creative Calendar

The third example in this section we've called the Creative Calendar. What does the mundane world of scheduling have to do with spiritual growth? There's an old cliché that gives us a clue: *All we've got is time.* How do we use our time? Could a practical look at our time and schedule aid us on our journey? In the movie, *Clean and Sober,* the hero of the movie shows up late to meet his sponsor, so late, in fact, the sponsor has had time to indulge his sugar addiction by drinking several malts. The sponsor comments wryly, "Addicts are always late." The comment brought laughs of recognition from the audience the night we saw the movie.

Do you have a problem being late? Do you have another issue that you can't seem to get a handle on? Use your writing skills to write a new behavior into your calendar. Here's how one person in a Twelve Step program talks about time and Steps Six and Seven.

> I was always late. I know it's a character defect. It's been clear for a long time. But how to deal with it? I tried praying to get out of the house on time. That didn't work. I asked why and the answer I received was this: I don't understand what "normal people" mean by time. I couldn't leave on time because I didn't know what it was. I left in time to get there if I made all the lights and there was a parking place by the door. I had a lead foot on the accelerator the whole way. It wasn't until

I had developed a serious collection of speeding tickets that I realized that prayer was not going to get me out the front door. I had to admit that I didn't understand time. When I got up in the morning, I tried to take a quick shower and emerged 30 minutes later. Shaving was a relaxed and reflective time for me. Then it was time for coffee, newspaper, and the Today Show. By the time I'd gone through my routine, it was already past time to get where I was going without speeding. I started writing down the time it took for me to get ready, not the time I thought it "should" take. I admitted, "I don't get it." Then I admitted, "I'll treat myself like a kid and make up a new schedule for new behavior." I thought the schedule was ridiculous: 45 minutes, shower and shaving, 30 minutes, coffee and newspaper, 15 minutes, get dressed, and 20 minutes for getting out the front door. Then I figured out when I had to get up to do all this and set my alarm much earlier. As I said, I thought it was ridiculous that I needed this much time, but I do need it.

I had prayed to have a character defect removed and it wasn't. What I got was learning to practice self-care in the morning. I learned that I *need* about two hours in the morning of leisurely time. Taking care of myself is the gift I needed. Being on time wasn't the issue. That took care of itself, once I saw the real issue. Getting places on time gives me a lot of serenity that I never had before and I'm getting used to its calmness. I'm even getting to like it better than the rush of speeding. You know, before sobriety, I thought that the great moments of life would be about work, fame, romance, great vacations. Now I've discovered I get choked up when I say, "We always go grocery shopping on Monday night." Who would believe it? I never had a routine before. I never had any predictability. I never knew a routine would give me such a deep sense of peace.

I thank my Higher Power every day for gradually letting me surrender to a routine.

Now take a minute or two and reflect on your known character defects. Which one could you work with by the Creative Calendar? One woman we know writes in a date with herself once a week to have a business meeting about money. If she doesn't write it down, she doesn't take care of the checkbook. Take out your calendar and write something on it that has never appeared before: a money date, a getting up earlier date, a time for exercising, a time for letter writing, or a Sunday morning appointment with your journal. Write in something you wish you would take the time for. After you've tried out your first date with yourself, you can decide whether the Creative Calendar could be useful to you. This process is especially helpful during times of stress when new behaviors may fall by the wayside. For example, the Christmas holidays are often stressful to people in recovery programs. You can use the Creative Calendar in several ways during the official holidays.

- Schedule in self-nurturing activities for you: taking a walk alone, meetings, going to work out. Write in these dates with yourself, officially.
- Write in your time limits for parties and get-togethers. For example: *"Caroling party at Jan's, 7-8:30."* This will help validate your new limits. If you are the first to leave the party, you can say, "I'm acting as a role model as an inner-directed person!" You could even write this as an affirmation on your calendar.

Writing New Rituals and Ceremonies

Many people in and out of Twelve Step programs have created and written new rituals. Perhaps this wave of ritual creation started in the 1960s when people started writing their own marriage ceremonies and when churches were involved in changing litanies and services, exploring the meaning of inclusive language.

What seems to be happening now is that people are creating new ceremonies as well as writing new words to old ceremonies. People are creating ceremonies for events that are not usually recognized in the larger culture. For example, people are creating ceremonies to celebrate the change of name, to acknowledge divorce, to celebrate sobriety and abstinence.

We can see evidence of this new ceremony making in several books. *The Inner Dance,* by Diane Mariechild, is a good resource on ceremonies. She offers guided meditations and thoughts about occasions we might celebrate. *Jambalaya: The Natural Woman's Book*, by Luisah Teish, is the story of her search to reclaim her ancient spiritual tradition from Africa and bring it to the New World. In *A Gradual Awakening,* Stephen Levine tells his story of how practicing Zen rituals changed his understanding of the world, life, and death. One of the most beautiful ceremonies described in a book is the ritual for name change in *The Courage to Heal: A Guide for Women Survivors of Child Sexual Abuse,* page 189.

What most of these ceremonies have in common is that they are down-to-earth and low-key. They share a dignified yet ordinary approach to ritual. In terms of language, the ceremonies share a grounding in ordinary speech. People talk from their daily speech, not from a lofty, inflated language.

If you would like to create your own ceremony, you might follow these steps.

Making a new ceremony is a lot like writing stage directions for a play. You need to consider, first, what is the occasion you'd like to celebrate. Fiftieth birthday? Divorce? Children out of the nest? Change of life? Sobriety? Choose an occasion. Now imagine the people who might be present. List your choices. Next, consider what you'd like to have happen. Here are possibilities:

- Invocation
- Singing
- Speeches
- Presentation of symbolic gifts
- Prayers
- Talking by all present
- Holding hands in a circle
- Lighting of candles
- Breaking bread together

Now you might make a rough draft of the actions you envision. Then it will be time to write. What do you want to say? What would you like others to say? Make a rough draft of your words. Now, let yourself enjoy a visual fantasy and imagine where this ceremony could take place. Out of doors? In a special room? Imagine the place and then imagine the objects that would give more meaning to the ceremony. What about a picture or an altar?

At a recent ceremony for their daughter's first birthday, a couple, Suzanne and Doug, created a ceremony to acknowledge their two friends' agreement to be godmothers. The ceremony, held in the backyard, included about twenty-five friends as participants who gathered for talking, singing, and welcoming. Everyone received the gift of a pine cone from a white pine, a symbolic gift, explained later during the ceremony. Both the mother and father talked about their daughter's first year of life and what they had learned.

Here is the father's talk. We thought it would be important to include it in order to stress that a ceremony can include *ordinary talking*.

A CEREMONY WELCOMING CYNTHIA AND
CATHARINE AS HANNAH'S GODMOTHERS:
SATURDAY, JUNE 18, 1988

Welcome:

We are happy that you could join our family — as
family — for this celebration of two events: Hannah's
birth one year ago, and Cindy and Cathy's "final vows"
as Hannah's godmothers.

The past year has been full of growth and change.
Today we are taking a deep breath to acknowledge
some of these achievements. Every day Hannah seems
to expand her abilities and confidence. She is now walking, exploring new sights all alone. Other changes
include strengthening the bonds with our new family.
This extends to Cindy and Cathy, all of you here this
afternoon, and others not able to attend.

As a parent, the aspect of this first year that has
been most surprising to me is how much time a baby
requires. Everyone said this who has been through it.
Yet, I was still overwhelmed. Fortunately, Cindy and
Cathy were close by and willing to help when we cried
out in need. Many times they have offered without
being asked.

It has been especially gratifying to watch the bonds
grow between Hannah and these two strong women.
That support and growth has brought all of us closer.
I thank Hannah for entering our lives, bringing us closer
as a family, and for all the joy she helps reveal to us
each day.

Cindy and Cathy were present to assist us at Hannah's
birth. They were a tremendous support team, helping
to keep us going through six hours of labor. While my
hands rarely broke contact with Suzanne's aching back,
Cindy and Cathy were there to provide us with sips

of juice, their essential emotional support, and cheers of encouragement.

A week ago, Cindy and Cathy were here again, assisting our ceremony planting a seven-year-old white pine tree in our front yard. It will grow strong and tall with the aid of nutrients from Hannah's placenta. We placed the young pine on top of these tissues where Hannah spent nine months, prior to her first breath, where she grew from a single cell into a baby ready to enter our world.

This is a time of year that brings many events for us to celebrate: Hannah's birth, a new moon, Cathy's birth, summer solstice, and Cindy and Cathy's third anniversary of commitment to one another. As we celebrate these events, we pause to show our gratitude to each of you for the support you have given us this first year of Hannah's life. We look forward to the mutual support that comes from our stronger bonds.

— Douglas Owens-Pike

Now that you have had a chance to reflect on one family's ceremony, write down the name of a ceremony you would like to have with your friends or family. Think about what you would like to say, and, before you go away from this chapter, write one paragraph for this ceremony; write out something you've never had the opportunity to say before.

We hope that this ceremony, and the other ideas in this chapter, will give you fresh ideas for ways that your writing can help you grow. The odds and ends collected here can lead only to more writing, and still more writing.

As you continue on your spiritual journey, may your writing continue to be a source of pleasure, clarity, discovery, and inspiration. May the blessings be.

Selected Bibliography

Alcoholics Anonymous (The Big Book), 3d ed. New York: Alcoholics Anonymous World Services, Inc., 1976.

Allen, Paula Gunn. *The Womanspirit Sourcebook.* Edited by Patrice Wynne. San Francisco: Harper & Row, 1988.

Baldwin, Christina. *One to One: Self-Understanding through Journal Writing.* New York: M. Evans and Company, 1977.

Bass, Ellen, and Laura Davis. *The Courage to Heal: A Guide for Women Survivors of Child Sexual Abuse.* New York: Harper & Row, 1988.

Beattie, Melody. *Codependent No More.* Center City, Minn.: Hazelden Educational Materials, 1987.

Bellow, Saul. *Herzog.* New York: Avon Books, 1961.

Block, Lawrence. *Write for Your Life.* Fort Myers Beach, Fla.: Write for Your Life, 1986.

Brande, Dorothea. *Becoming a Writer.* San Diego: Harcourt, Brace & Co., 1934.

Caddy, John. *The Color of Mesabi Bones.* Minneapolis: Milkweed Editions, 1989.

Capacchione, Linda. *The Creative Journal, The Art of Finding Yourself.* Ohio University Press, 1979.

Cardinal, Marie. *The Words to Say It.* Cambridge, Mass.: Van Vactor & Goodheart, Inc., 1983.

Carver, Raymond. *Where Water Comes Together with Other Water.* New York: Random House, 1984.

Day, Sharon, and Pat Panagoulias. *Drink the Winds, Let the Waters Flow Free.* Minneapolis: Johnson Institute, Inc., 1983.

Dickinson, Emily. *The Life and Letters of Emily Dickinson.* By Martha Gilbert Dickinson Bianchi, 1924.

Eckhart, Meister. *Breakthrough: Meister Eckhart's Creation Spirituality in New Translation*. Introduction and Commentaries by Matthew Fox. Garden City, N.Y.: Image Books, 1980.

Edwards, Betty. *Drawing from the Right Side of the Brain*. Los Angeles: J.P. Tarcher, Inc., 1979.

Elbow, Peter. *Writing Without Teachers*. New York: Oxford University Press, 1973.

Elytis, Odysseas. *The Little Mariner*. Port Townsend, Wash.: Copper Canyon Press, 1988.

Fox, Matthew. *Original Blessing*. Santa Fe, N. Mex.: Bear & Company, 1983.

Gawain, Shakti. *Creative Visualization*. New York: Bantam Books, Inc., 1982.

Goldberg, Natalie. *Writing Down the Bones*. Boston and London: Shambhala, 1986.

Green, Kate. *If the World Is Running Out*. Minneapolis: Holy Cow! Press, 1983.

Hall, Nor. *The Moon & the Virgin*. New York: Harper & Row, 1982.

Hanson, Phebe. *Sacred Hearts*. Minneapolis: Milkweed Editions, 1985.

Henricks, Gay, and Russel Wills. *The Centering Book: Awareness Activities for Children, Parents, and Teachers*. Englewood Cliffs, N.J.: Prentice-Hall, Inc., 1975.

Hyde, Lewis. *The Gift, Imagination and the Erotic Life of Property*. New York: Vintage Books, 1979.

Jung, Carl G. *The Portable Jung*, Joseph Campbell, ed. New York: The Viking Press, 1971.

Kafka, Franz. *Letter to His Father*. New York: Schocken Books, 1953.

Larkin, Joan. *A Long Sound*. Penobscot, Maine: Granite Press, 1986.

Larson, Earnie. *Stage II Relationships: Love Beyond Addiction*. San Francisco: Harper & Row, 1982.

Levine, Stephen. *A Gradual Awakening*, 1979.

Lloyd, Roseann. *Tap Dancing for Big Mom.* St. Paul, Minn.: New Rivers Press, 1986.

Mallon, Thomas. *A Book of One's Own: People and Their Diaries.* New York: Ticknor & Fields, 1984.

Mariechild, Diane. *Mother Wit: A Feminist Guide to Psychic Development.* Trumansburg, New York: The Crossing Press, 1981.

_____. *The Inner Dance: A Guide to Spiritual and Psychological Unfolding.* Freedom, Calif.: The Crossing Press, 1987.

Miller, Alice. *Thou Shalt Not Be Aware: Society's Betrayal of the Child.* New York: Farra Straus Giroux, 1984.

Moffat, Mary Jane and Charlotte Painter. *Revelations: Diaries of Women.* New York: Random House, 1975.

Morrison, Toni. *Beloved.* New York: Alfred A. Knopf, 1987.

Nelson, Victoria. *Writer's Block and How To Use It.* Cincinnati: Writers Digest Books, 1985.

Nin, Anaïs. *The Diary of Anaïs Nin.* Vol. 1, 1931-1934. Edited by Gunther Stuhlman. New York: Swallow Press, Harcourt, Brace & Co., Inc., 1966.

Olds, Sharon. *The Dead and the Living.* New York: Alfred A. Knopf, 1984.

Pagels, Elaine. *The Gnostic Gospels.* New York: Vintage Books, 1981.

Ponder, Catherine. *The Dynamic Laws of Prosperity.* Englewood Cliffs, N.J.: Prentice-Hall, Inc., 1962.

Progoff, Ira. *Depth Psychology and Modern Man.* New York: McGraw-Hill Book Co., 1959.

Rainer, Tristine. *The New Diary.* Los Angeles: Jeremy P. Tarcher, Inc., 1978.

Ray, Sondra. *Loving Relationships.* Berkeley, Calif.: Celestial Arts, 1980.

Rilke, Rainer Maria. *Stories of God.* New York: W. W. Norton & Co., 1963.

Robertson, Nan. *Getting Better: Inside Alcoholics Anonymous.* New York: William Morrow and Company, Inc., 1988.

Soto, Gary. *The Elements of San Joaquin*. Pittsburgh: The University of Pittsburgh Press, 1977.

Teish, Louisah. *Jambalaya: The Natural Woman's Book of Personal Charms and Practical Rituals*. San Francisco: Harper & Row, 1985.

_____. *The Womanspirit Sourcebook*. Edited by Patrice Wynne. San Francisco: Harper & Row, 1988.

The Twelve Steps for Everyone (Who Really Wants Them). Minneapolis: CompCare, 1983.

Today's Gift. Center City, Minn.: Hazelden Educational Materials, 1985.

Ueland, Brenda. *If You Want to Write*. St. Paul, Minn.: The Schubert Club, 1984.

V., Rachel. *A Woman Like You*. San Francisco: Harper & Row, 1985.

Walker, Alice. *The Color Purple*. New York: Harcourt Brace Jovanovich, 1982.

Whitman, Walt. *Leaves of Grass*. New York: The Modern Library, Random House, following the edition of 1891-92.

Wholey, Dennis. *The Courage to Change*. Large Print Edition. Boston: G. K. Hall & Co., 1985.

Wright, James. *The Branch Will Not Break*. Middletown, Conn.: Wesleyan University Press, 1961.

THE TWELVE STEPS OF ALCOHOLICS ANONYMOUS*

1. We admitted we were powerless over alcohol—that our lives had become unmanageable.

2. Came to believe that a Power greater than ourselves could restore us to sanity.

3. Made a decision to turn our will and our lives over to the care of God *as we understood him.*

4. Made a searching and fearless moral inventory of ourselves.

5. Admitted to God, to ourselves, and to another human being the exact nature of our wrongs.

6. Were entirely ready to have God remove all these defects of character.

7. Humbly asked Him to remove our shortcomings.

8. Made a list of all persons we had harmed, and became willing to make amends to them all.

9. Made direct amends to such people wherever possible, except when to do so would injure them or others.

10. Continued to take personal inventory and when we were wrong promptly admitted it.

11. Sought through prayer and meditation to improve our conscious contact with God *as we understood Him,* praying only for knowledge of His will for us and the power to carry that out.

12. Having had a spiritual awakening as the result of these steps, we tried to carry this message to alcoholics, and to practice these principles in all our affairs.

*The Twelve Steps of A.A. are taken from *Alcoholics Anonymous* (Third Edition), published by A.A. World Services, Inc., New York, N.Y., 59-60. Reprinted with permission.

Index

Other titles that will interest you...

Stairway to Serenity
The Eleventh Step
  Stairway to Serenity is a down-to-earth guide for finding serenity in spiritual growth. The author describes how, through the Eleventh Step, we can discover a peace of mind greater than any "high" we found in addiction. 92 pp.
Order No. 5051

The Promise of a New Day
  by Karen Casey and Martha Vanceburg
  Written in the tradition of *Each Day a New Beginning*, this guide reaches out to all people who seek full, healthy living. For anyone seeking greater rewards in daily life, this meditation book affirms our strengths and gives us hope and peace. 400 pp.
Order No. 1045

Communication Skills
  by Richard S.
  With this pamphlet, we can learn how to be better listeners, talk about our own needs, and learn other skills that can help us build more intimate relationships with others. 20 pp.
Order No. 5566
